addict

*Do not be anxious about tomorrow;
tomorrow will look after itself.
Each day has troubles enough of
its own.*
                              —*Matthew 6:34*

addict
a doctor's odyssey

DR. JAMES DEWITT WITH AL HIRSHBERG

Cowles Book Company, Inc.
A subsidiary of Henry Regnery Company
Chicago

Dedicated to Our Children

Preface

About two weeks ago, the phone rang and Doris said, "the call is for you, Jim. Ed Cass is on the phone".

I picked up the phone. "Hi, Ed, how are you doing?"

"Good," he replied, then continued, "Jim, I'd like to ask you to do a personal favor for me. I know how busy you are and this will probably take a whole morning of your time, so—what the hell—it won't change our friendship if you can't work it in."

"I hope I can, what's the favor?".

"I'd really be grateful if you could find the time to speak at the high school my two daughters attend in Roslindale. In fact, as we've both said many times, you and I not only have to give honest answers, we must also volunteer the truth in order to reach our goals. Here it is, I already called the school. If you could, they'd like you to come out next Wednesday morning and speak to half the school at about 9:30 A.M. and the other half about 10:45 A.M. The auditorium will only seat half of the students at a time."

"One second," I said, as I glanced at my claendar. "Wonderful, I'm clear all that morning." Then Ed asked me if I could be at his office at 9:00 A.M. the following Wednesday so he could drive us both out to the school. Ed would introduce me and talk about drugs for fifteen minutes, then I would have about forty-five minutes to speak to the assembly.

After saying goodbye to Ed, Doris and I talked about what he said and how proud and happy we were that Ed would want me to lecture at his daughters' school.

As I resumed my work a feeling I could not comprehend came over me. I started to get more and more depressed and within a couple of hours I was really miserable—not scared, not anxious, but really depressed and miserable. Finally, I understood my depression as clearly and logically as any feeling could be understood.

Ed and I had been good friends since I met him at the Region I headquarters of the Federal Bureau of Narcotics and Dangerous Drugs about four years ago. I decided I was ready to try to get back my Massachusetts medical and narcotics license. He went over my records and said, "I think you can make it Jim! It is up to the State but we won't send a report that might hold you back." As I left the office, he said, "Keep in touch with me. Drop in and say hello if you're downtown!" I knew he meant those words, so I did call him and did drop in many times, usually because everything I tried to do in the next few years was blocked somewhere along the line. When Ed wasn't there I would talk with Agent Joe Gately, whom I came to admire a great deal. Occasionally, Dick Callahan, then Regional Director, took a few minutes to shoot the breeze with me, a junkie who just dropped in.

One time in particular I remember calling Ed, now Regional Director, to ask him if he knew Sgt. Dan Delaney of the State Police. Ed was not there so I asked to speak with Joe Gately. I told Joe that Sgt. Delaney and his boys had just left my apartment. They had received a false report about me and, in following it up, had spent two and a half hours questioning me about my treatment of junkies. The police left on friendly terms but I was still shook up.

Joe said that Ed was out of town but I would be able to reach him the following morning. Joe then said, "I know this won't help you very much, but try not to worry. You are treating junkies to the best of your ability. Personally, I think you're ok. Call Ed tomorrow." It helped a lot.

While waiting to call Ed I thought back to the first time I had called him after receiving my medical and narcotics license. I asked him if he knew of any place that would accept a sick junkie, who had just called me from Lowell. He knew of no place except Boston State and Bridgewater. The junkie had tried Boston State and found a mile-long waiting list for their twenty-bed withdrawl ward and he did not want to go to Bridgewater.

Ed asked how things were going. "Good," I replied, "but everything I try to do seems to have a thousand obstacles in the way." I could sense his disappointment and realized he would go all out to help a person who was trying to do something he believed in.

When I told Ed about Sgt. Delaney's investigation, he said, "over the years, Dan and I have done a lot of work together. When Dan said he believed in your work, you can count on his 100 percent support. Dan never says things just to be polite."

I breathed a sigh of relief.

The troubles were still there, an eviction notice, warrants issued for my arrest because I failed to make payments on a loan I had made in order to stay in practice. The facts remained but I once more had the knowledge every junkie must have that he is not quite alone. Doris and I began to gain this knowledge years before while in a car with Father Bill Carrigg. I'm sure our faith was strengthened by the many hours spent with Father Walter Lennon, Rev. Jim McCloy, Father Neil Harrington, and State Senators Bill Saltonstall, and Kevin Harrington. All these people have enough faith in me to encourage me to write this book. When I told each one I would bring him a copy of the manuscript before it was published, he said, "No. You are too busy now, I'll read it in the book."

Anyone reading this book can be sure he will travel a bit of the pathological road every junkie is guaranteed: a road built by the symptoms of his disastrous disease; a road with an unknown destination. Since this disease is incurable I know that I am not cured, only that my disease has been arrested. All the good people I have mentioned cannot control my tomorrows. But with faith in God, faith in myself, faith in my wife Doris, and the knowledge that I am not quite alone, I can control my own tomorrows and be reborn each day into another twenty-four hours that starts when I awake and say "Thy will be done" and ends when I get on my knees and thank God for another drug-free day.

addict

I

IT started innocently enough in the town of Brewer, Maine, one autumn afternoon in 1953. Brewer is a lovely little community, not far from Bangor, and well located medically because it is within easy range of three hospitals—the Eastern Maine General in Bangor, of whose staff I was a member, the Central Maine General in Lewiston, and the Maine General in Portland. My wife, Kay, who also acted as my secretary and office assistant, lived with me in a huge barn of a place, an ancient, rambling, multigabled edifice that looked haunted in the gathering dark of the evening, as if designed by Charles Addams. This 135-year-old house, with fifteen rooms and three baths, was a maze of corridors, staircases, and odd little doors in odd little places. In the three years I lived there, I doubt if I ever managed to see every nook and corner of it, or to find the sources of all its squeaks and creaks (often characteristics of charming old New England mansions). It was the central point of fifty acres of forest on the Penobscot River: a hunter's paradise, the answer to a fisherman's dream.

I had a good practice in the district, and perfect facilities for recreation in my leisure hours. I knew everyone in town and everyone knew me—a young giant of a man, six feet four inches tall, 250 pounds, proud of my strength and agility acquired through a lifelong love of sports that nearly landed

1

me in professional baseball instead of medicine. At the age of seventeen, when I finished high school, I had been offered a contract by one of the farm clubs of the New York Yankees. Tempting as the offer was, I had turned it down in favor of a basketball scholarship to Mount Union College in Alliance, Ohio, not far from the Akron suburb where I grew up. Even then, I had wanted to become a doctor, an ambition that had the enthusiastic approval of my father, a tall, gaunt, gentle man who for years was superintendent of a regional high school. He became a local living legend when a new school in Cuyahoga Falls was named after him. He once told me that he had sometimes toyed with the idea of becoming a doctor himself, and to this day he relives in me the life he would have chosen if the academic field had been less appealing to him.

My life was busy both in and out of medicine. My general practice followed a rotating internship at the Eastern Maine Hospital and was augmented by three months of graduate study in obstetrics at the Providence Lying-In. I wanted to specialize in obstetrics and, in fact, had already been accepted for a year of residency in a Cleveland hospital beginning in July, 1954.

Much of my spare time was spent hunting in season, mostly on my own property. In the company of friends or my little girl Karen, and sometimes alone, I had spent the early part of October, 1953, outdoors with my dogs whenever I could find a lull in my practice. My woods were alive with pheasant, partridge, and woodcock. I usually took an English setter I had trained myself or a German pointer I had helped to train. We had other dogs, too, including a pet spaniel for Karen, our only child at the time. As a tiny girl, Karen loved to go out into those woods with me. Later, she became as enthusiastic a hunter and lover of the outdoors as I was myself. She could handle a rifle almost as soon as she was big enough to lift one.

It was a passion for hunting that led me to Maine in the first place. While attending George Washington University Medical School, I worked a few summers in the Adirondacks, and during those summers I occasionally went trout fishing with a retired detective from New York City who had a camp in Maine. This man aroused my interest in the wild, woody environs of Bangor, and I fell in love with the area on sight. My fondness for that area led to my decision to do my internship at Eastern Maine General and when my internship was completed to make a down payment on the property in Brewer, where I hoped to establish a permanent residence for myself and my family. The place had seemed to offer us a good life and the opportunity for me to establish the type of practice I thought I would enjoy —part country doctor, part obstetrics specialist.

If not for an incident that occurred one autumn afternoon in 1953, Brewer would have given us everything I had hoped for. If not for that incident, I would probably still be hunting pheasant, partridge, and woodcock on my own property to-day. If not for that incident, I would very likely have grown gray in the obscurity of the small town and the woods I loved, blissfully unaware of the pitfalls and sophisticated problems of the alcoholism and drug addiction that would turn my life upside down, and indeed, nearly end it in a gutter in Boston's mangy South End. If not for that incident, I would have spared myself and those closest to me years of agony, loneliness, shame, and disgrace. If any good at all came from that incident, it was the chance to find happiness with a wonderful companion and to provide myself with a goal in life totally devoid of the selfish motives that had drawn me to Maine.

I had set off a couple of rooms in my home as an office where I saw patients in the afternoon following my usual morning hospital rounds. My fee, four dollars for house calls, three for office visits, was consistent with the fees of most doctors in the area. As nurse, secretary, receptionist, and general assistant, Kay took care of all the details, such as registering new patients and scheduling appointments for old ones. On the day that changed my life, I was holding routine office hours. I had just begun to examine one patient in the treatment room, with about ten others in the waiting room, when I had a phone call from a woman whose baby I had delivered about four months earlier. Except during her pregnancy, which was normal, I rarely saw her or her husband. Both were about twenty-five years old, they attended the same church we did, and friendly greetings there constituted our entire relationship.

Her call was our first direct contact since I had discharged her as a patient after her child was born. Although sounding reasonably calm on the phone, she was obviously upset because her husband had suddenly become quite ill.

"He can hardly talk," she said. "He isn't able to move his arms or legs, seems almost completely paralyzed, and I'm sure he's running a high fever."

"How high?" I asked.

"I don't know. I haven't a thermometer, but he feels terribly hot and his muscles are twitching."

"I'll be right out," I said.

I asked Kay to explain the circumstances to the waiting patients and to reschedule their appointments; then I got my bag, took it to the car, and started on Route Nine toward Bucksport. The road, a typical backwoods tar-covered two-lane highway, was fairly clear of traffic, and I made the five miles or so between my house and the patient's in seven or eight minutes. My first thought was of polio, since we had had a good deal of it that summer. No effective vaccine for polio had yet been developed, and that was everyone's first thought when paralysis appeared to be a factor in a new illness. But as always when I started on an unexpected house call, I left my mind open until I could examine the patient.

The house was old and, although smaller, as typical of eighteenth-century New England architecture as my own home. After the wife, who was very distraught, let me inside, I tried to talk to her husband, who was lying down in a bedroom at the head of a steep staircase. It was impossible to carry on a conversation with the man. His forehead was burning, his muscles twitching, his voice inaudible; he was delirious. Before putting a thermometer in his mouth I asked why he thought he was paralyzed, but all he could do was to make meaningless lip movements. While taking his temperature, I tested his reflexes; although they were normal, showing no brain irritation, his temperature had soared to 106°. I no longer suspected polio, because it rarely causes such a high fever, especially in the absence of reflex changes, but I wanted to get him to the hospital as quickly as possible. Even with normal reflexes, you never know what you might be facing with a 106° temperature. There is always the possibility of convulsions, and there is no way of accurately determining the cause of the fever without laboratory tests, which can be made only at the hospital. In addition to this, I was concerned about signs of tetanus from increasingly heavy breathing.

I got the man to swallow four aspirins, then phoned a Brewer funeral home because it had the only ambulance service in town. The owner told me he was alone and couldn't come out without a driver because it would take two men to get the patient out of the house and into the ambulance on a stretcher. In desperation, for the man was very ill, I explained that this was an emergency and that I was strong enough to help him move the sick man. Finally, the owner of the ambulance agreed to come. In the interim I tried to reassure the woman that her husband almost surely had neither polio nor meningitis, and might very well be suffering from nothing more than a severe virus infection, which could quickly be cured.

By the time the funeral director arrived, the patient, a big, solidly built man, was unconscious, an absolutely dead weight to be moved down the stairway beneath a ceiling so low that I had had to bend down in order to climb it. We had no trouble getting the man from the bed to the stretcher, which we put on the floor. However, there was nothing with which to strap him in securely, so we had to hold him as well as the stretcher as we worked our way down the stairs, the funeral director leading the way, holding his feet, while I held his head. I was in a very awkward position, bent over, not only to keep my head from hitting the ceiling, but to keep the patient from tumbling down on the man below. Although steep, the stairway wasn't long, perhaps a dozen or fifteen steps. But it was an ordeal moving from one step to the next. When we finally got the patient down and into the back of the ambulance, I felt no pain—only relief that the difficult job was done. The possibility of self-injury never occurred to me as I followed the ambulance into town. The incident appeared to be just another part of the day's work.

The man's fever had subsided a little when we reached the hospital, but he needed immediate carbon dioxide for his tetanus, and his heavy breathing was much more intense. At about this time I began having leg pains, not too severe at first, but gradually becoming worse. I dismissed these pains as a temporary condition caused by my awkward position while helping to carry the patient downstairs. Still, while working on him in the emergency room of the hospital, I was reminded of the previous day, when I had helped a friend roll up a heavy link chain fence and put it into his station wagon to take to a new home he had bought in Bangor. Although this had caused me no pain at the time, it could, I now realized, have weakened my back to a point where something might have been likely to "give" under additional strain.

However, I continued to work on the patient (finally convinced that my optimistic guess of a virus infection was correct), injected him with penicillin, and called to reassure his wife, who had stayed home with her children. With that off my mind, I suddenly became aware that my pain, steadily increasing, had become so severe that I had to get off my feet. I went into an adjoining room to lie down on a stretcher. Despite the pain, I took the whole thing lightly. *Nothing can ever stop me*, I thought, *nothing is big enough. I'm too tall, too strong, in too good condition to be hurt simply by going downstairs at the back end of a stretcher.*

The head nurse from the emergency room happened to look in as she walked by, and asked me what was wrong.

"I guess I'm going into a coma," I said lightly. "Maybe I'm dying. Better start some plasma."

"Come on, doctor," she said. "Don't kid me. This isn't like you at all."

"Well, I have a little pain in my leg. I'm just going to lie here until it eases up, and then I think I'll go home."

Another doctor—a close friend—also stopped in when he saw me on the stretcher.

"Hey, Jim," he called. "What are you doing?"

"I've got a disc," I said, partly serious, partly in fun.

"What do you mean?"

"Just what I said. I've got a good sciatic pain down my

right leg. It'll quiet down. When it does, I'll go home and relax in a hot tub."

"It's impossible. How did you get it?"

"Helping to carry a guy on a stretcher down a flight of stairs," I said. "I guess I got on the wrong end."

We both laughed, and he went on his way. But as I continued to lie there, I began to realize that this wasn't half as funny as I had thought at first. A hard, radiating pain was shooting up and down my right leg and becoming progressively worse all the time. This sort of pain is one sign of a possible disc problem. It can be hours before the back actually starts hurting because the nerve roots originating in the spinal cord and supplying the leg sometimes bear the early brunt of pressure. The longer I lay there, the surer I was that this was what was happening to me, yet I couldn't believe it and wouldn't submit to it. I had been hurt before, although never seriously—I had twice broken an arm in football and had been hit several times while boxing when I served in the navy during World War II—and had always been proud of my higher-than-average tolerance for pain. Now, while still in the emergency room, I began to feel the pain in my back, and when it intensified there, I decided to drive home while I could still function. It was half an hour since I had gotten onto the stretcher, and now I struggled off to phone Kay. I told her I had a little back spasm from helping to carry a patient, and asked her to cancel any more afternoon appointments. By the time I left the hospital, I had been gone about two and a half hours, so even if I hadn't been hurt there would have been no time to see more than one or two patients.

I drove home—in agony—and got into the tub, which was ready when I arrived. I stayed in there about twenty minutes, but the pain only became worse—so much worse that Kay had to help me out. Sure that I had a herniated intervertebral disc somewhere in the lumbar region of my back, I called Dr. Carl Irwin, a neurosurgeon on our Eastern General staff, and he came immediately. By 9:30 that night I was back in the hospital, this time as a patient.

In plain, nonmedical English, my condition is commonly known as a ruptured disc, the type suffered by thousands of people, many of whom need surgery to correct it. There is a disc between each of the vertebrae that form the backbone. A disc is a segment of cartilage that acts as a cushion between vertebrae to keep the bones from rubbing together, functioning in much the same way as a gasket. There are discs in all three major regions of the spine: cervical (neck), thoracic (chest), and lumbar (lower back). The most commonly ruptured disc, the one usually ruptured as a result of undue strain such as I had undergone, is in the lumbar region, where the sciatic nerve starts (that nerve goes all the way down to the outside part of the foot). When a disc ruptures, it moves out far enough to touch the sciatic nerve, causing that to swell and become extremely irritated. Although the source of the trouble is in your back, your brain tells you that one or both of your legs are affected, and intense leg pain (mine was in the right leg) results. Any advanced medical student can diagnose a probable ruptured lumbar disc, so my self-diagnosis required no unusual amount of medical astuteness.

Since bed rest can relieve the condition, doctors were reluctant to operate in those days and are even more reluctant to do so now. While the rate of surgical success is high—approximately 80 percent—there is still about a 20 percent chance that complications will arise that might require further surgery or, in a very small percentage of cases, that permanent and incorrectable leg paralysis will result. Generally, however, although not as routine as, say, an appendectomy or a hernia operation, disc surgery is not considered particularly dangerous. Medical conservatism in this case is simply based upon the undeniable fact that bed rest, although it might take longer, is always preferable to surgery.

Therefore, as a matter of routine, Dr. Irwin at first prescribed bed rest for me. X rays showed the probability of a ruptured disc, although it takes a mylogram to confirm the diagnosis (if a patient seems to be coming along well, medical men avoid a mylogram, as that procedure is complicated and sometimes painful). Besides, improvement by bed rest may mean that what appears to be a ruptured disc is actually nothing more than a muscle spasm, which can be eliminated by immobilizing the patient for a week to ten days.

During my first few days in the hospital, when my leg pains were acute, I was given codeine or Demerol; later, when the pain diminished, aspirin was sufficient to keep me comfortable. During my first hospital stay, I improved so much that the doctor let me go home after ten days. We had both thought that I had a ruptured disc, but he decided to forego a mylogram, and I felt so good when I left the hospital that I was ready to believe we had been wrong. I looked forward to resuming my practice, continuing my hunting, and going on to Cleveland in July to take up a year's residency in obstetrics.

Kay came to pick me up in the station wagon. Although we had a bumpy ride home, I felt fine when we arrived. I decided to take it easy that night, then to begin my regular routine with hospital rounds the next morning. I slept well and had only slight pain at the hospital in the morning. But while examining patients in my home office during the afternoon, my right leg began bothering me again. In the evening the pain became worse, and after a night of intense discomfort I phoned Carl Irwin, who told me to go back to the hospital. I remained in agony as Kay drove me in, but when I arrived, I struggled out, got into a waiting wheelchair, and was checked in as a patient once again.

This time, after X rays still showed signs of a herniated disc, Carl ordered a mylogram, preceded by a local anesthetic. Once that has taken effect, spinal fluid is drawn out and a radiopaque dye is inserted with a large needle. While this process was somewhat uncomfortable, I didn't mind it because I had already suffered much worse pain. The only actual pain in a mylogram comes when the dye is withdrawn, for that changes the pressure on the spinal cord; this is also the only dangerous part of the procedure because, since it's impossible to get out all the dye, there is a very slight chance of some getting into the brain and causing damage. However, this happens so seldom that the procedure is considered virtually 100 percent safe, as it was in my case.

If there had been any doubt before about my disc's being ruptured, it was quickly dispelled by the mylogram, which confirmed our original diagnosis. My pain now was so hard and constant that I was glad Carl decided to operate, which he did in late November, 1953, about a month after I first injured my back. Doctors today are inclined to wait longer, in the hope that bed rest will still do the job, but I felt that Carl's decision was right—I would have recommended surgery for a patient of my own under the same circumstances.

In disc surgery, there is usually the option of cutting away the part of the disc that touches the sciatic nerve and making it level with the vertebrae involved (mine are medically known as L-3 and L-4, the third and fourth down from the top of the lumbar region) or, if most of the disc seems to be herniated (protruding), of fusing together the two vertebrae after eliminating the disc. Most doctors prefer not to fuse because that has the effect of making one vertebra out of two, thus restricting a certain amount of motor activity. Besides, since all of the disc is rarely in view, a fusion must be done blindly; there's no way of determining just how much usable disc may be left between the two vertebrae.

In my case, Dr. Irwin did a levelling operation rather than a fusion. That, too, was (and often still is) normal procedure; I had assisted at many disc operations involving patients of my own, and fusions were done only when it appeared to be absolutely necessary. If I had been a witness to my own operation in Bangor, I'm sure I would have been in agreement with Carl's decision—with proper rest and care, the operation he performed should have been enough to correct the problem.

The operation appeared successful, and I had a normal hospital convalescence of about ten days, followed by a few weeks of rest at home, both in bed and out. By the middle of January, 1954, free of hard pain, I resumed my normal activities, with a few slight modifications to compensate for my generally weakened condition. For one thing, I had to eliminate one part of my practice: my job as the regular physician for the Eastern Corporation, a mill in Brewer where I would previously go two days a week to treat routine injuries, and be on call for emergencies, some of which came at night. Also, because it was now dangerous for me to bear the weight of a shotgun or rifle, I traded mine in for a .45-caliber Colt revolver and a .22-caliber pistol. I could still run my dogs and shoot an occasional rabbit, but few birds. Small-arms accuracy is consistently good only at shorter distances than I was used to; you can rarely get close enough to a bird to hit it with anything lighter than a shotgun.

Thinking that I was headed for complete recovery—I should have known there would always be some limitations—

I wasn't as careful a patient as I would have been a doctor. When the weeks went by with no apparent recurrence of my back problem, I became more and more active. While this was natural, since nobody as energetic as I had formerly been is inclined to treat himself as an invalid, it was also dangerous. Carl had warned me to take plenty of time—as much as a year, if necessary—before resuming anything resembling my normal schedule. But that was like trying to put reins on a wild horse. Except for giving up the Eastern Corporation job and swapping rifles for small arms, I was soon doing everything in my usual manner—not as much due to ignorance as to false optimism. With a trick back, I should have realized I would always have to be careful; anticipating a complete recovery was senseless and unrealistic. Within a few weeks after I got home, I began refusing to coddle myself or to admit that there was anything I would never be able to do safely again.

I managed fairly well until about mid-March. Then the pain—identical to that which had plagued me before the operation—began coming back. I tried to ignore it at first, largely, I think, because I wouldn't believe that it could happen so soon after surgery. Also, the time for me to take that year of obstetrics residency in Cleveland was getting closer. Anyway, I didn't mention my pain to anyone, least of all Carl Irwin, the one person I should have told. I knew he would have insisted upon my returning to the hospital, where I might have been immobilized indefinitely and possibly have undergone further surgery, which would have prevented me from accepting the residency I so badly wanted. I didn't tell Kay, either, because, pregnant with Doug, our second child, who was due in early June, she had enough on her mind. The only solution I could think of was the worst thing I could have ever done—making a self-diagnosis and prescribing pain-killing drugs for myself. Codeine has always nauseated me, but it is usually effective against pain and not too strong, so I began with codeine, in smaller-than-normal doses. The normal dosage is about a grain every three or four hours; I started on a quarter grain, taking it by mouth. When that failed to help, I went to half a grain. I didn't think of the possibility of addiction, especially from such a modest beginning.

Before I went to medical school, the only addict I had ever known of was a doctor in Ohio, who, although a first-class diagnostician, was often, in the words of my father, "sick." Years later, my father told me he had become an addict, probably through exposure to narcotics. I think that was the only time my parents had ever known a real, live addict before my own addiction began, but he was such a good doctor that they nevertheless used him when he was available.

Although I had been warned in medical school of the danger of addiction in prescribing certain drugs, I knew very little about it; I hadn't had much experience with it and, in fact, took the popular stand, maintaining that, rather than being a sickness, addiction was an inexcusable vice, preventable to the extent that no addict had anyone to blame for his troubles but himself. However, I wasn't as severe in my attitude towards drug or alcohol addicts as were some of my colleagues and friends. I felt sorry for the first addicts I ever saw at close range, in the Washington, D.C., hospitals where I worked while attending medical school. Through books, patients, professors, and fellow workers, all medical students become aware of the possibility of addiction to strong pain-killing narcotics, particularly Demerol and morphine (the most powerful and addictive legal drug in this country).

While I was attending medical school in the late 1940s,

after I got out of the navy, Washington was either the first or second city in the country in per capita use of heroin (at this writing Boston now holds that dubious distinction). As students, our interest lay more in the medical effects of addiction than in addiction itself. We did learn a little about treating withdrawal, but there wasn't much to learn about that at the time, because nobody was sure how best to handle withdrawal. Some doctors believed in cold turkey withdrawal whereby the patient just went through his agony without any medication; others believed in gradually getting the patient through by administering, in decreasing amounts, less addictive drugs than he had been taking. This latter method, which is less severe than cold turkey but takes longer, is how nonaddicts are eased off morphine legitimately given to relieve pain, and it works well. In fact, since this type of patient ordinarily takes whatever medication he is given without asking questions, he usually is unaware that he is being given anything to prevent possible addiction; after recovery, he often doesn't even know that he might have been exposed to it.

During my medical school days, our interest in withdrawal was not as important to us as the study of side effects of addiction, which can be fatal. The most common cause of death is simply forgetting to sterilize the needle before shooting, thereby exposing the incautious addict to such ailments as bacterial endocarditis, infections of the heart lining, and liver or kidney problems. Often, we didn't even know that many patients with these afflictions were addicts until we took their histories; even then, we were never sure unless they admitted it directly. Many didn't. Despite the amount of heroin and number of junkies in the city, addiction was still something of a rarity and few were willing to discuss the subject with reference to themselves.

Although I had some empathy with addicted people, I never had much patience with them. I inherited a few alcoholics and drug addicts when I began my general practice in Bangor, mostly because other doctors didn't want to bother with them. Sometimes, frantic calls would come in the middle of the night. When I got up to answer them Kay would ask, "What is it?," and I'd say, "Another damn alcoholic," or "Another damn dope addict." I really didn't know just how to treat either and had trouble trying to learn because there were only a handful in the area. Alcoholics were most difficult for me because I had never had any previous contact with them. When I tried to help the few junkies I saw, I used the techniques we used at medical school. Once in a while I saw victims of barbiturate poisoning. I was surprised to learn that barbiturates in overdoses were not the only nonnarcotic drugs capable of causing brain damage—people who used Doriden or Miltown as tranquilizers, because they imagined that drugs without a barbiturate base were safe, ran the same risks. Taken in small enough quantities these drugs might be safe enough, but to some heavy users they were as lethal as barbiturates and even more addictive.

As my pain persisted through the spring of 1954, I took codeine in increasing quantities until I went beyond the normal dosage. No one, not even Kay, knew, since I used it only at night, hoping that it would ease the pain enough to let me sleep. When it failed to do this, and nauseated me as much as it ever had, I knew I had to choose one of two alternatives—either to see Carl Irwin and let him hospitalize me, or to go to a stronger drug. I definitely didn't want to see Carl, or any other doctor, for fear of losing my Cleveland residency, now only a couple of months away. I decided I could stand the pain enough to continue working until it was time to leave for Ohio—if I could only find something which would knock me out at night. With codeine eliminated, I moved on to Demerol, considered so strong that some doctors prescribe it only on alternate days. The usual practice is to administer fifty or a hundred milligrams (one or two tablets) every three hours one day, and hope that that would suffice to carry the patient through the next without too much distress. It rarely does, but it is considered better for a patient to suffer a little than to risk addiction.

Still taking it only at bedtime, I started slowly on Demerol, one tablet at a time. This dosage snowballed quickly, because such a small amount didn't do anything for the pain. Soon I was taking a couple of hundred milligrams four or five times a night and still not getting any relief. The more maddening the pain in my back and legs became the less I thought about the possibility of addiction. I began to figure out new ways to get extra Demerol, since I was using it faster than I could prescribe it for patients. One of the easiest methods was to pester private nurses on part-time duty in homes where patients were suffering from severe ailments. I would stop by in the morning before making my hospital rounds and question a nurse about how much pain her patient had. If she answered, "Little," or, "None," I would keep repeating the same question until she finally agreed that perhaps there was more pain than she thought. Then I would tell her that I'd stop in again en route to my home with enough Demerol to last a few days. I did that with three or· four patients a day, going to a different home each day in order to keep the nurses from becoming suspicious. After each morning visit I went to a drugstore, careful not to go to the same one too often, and ordered a hundred tablets of Demerol; I then left a few off at each house and kept the rest. Eventually, I put the patient on morphine (which, especially in cases of terminal cancer, is done routinely) and kept ordering Demerol as well. It was the kind of switch a doctor can get away with—although not for long, because sooner or later either a nurse or a druggist will become suspicious.

I did everything I could to obtain drugs for myself without causing suspicion. Sometimes I wrote prescriptions for non-existent patients; sometimes I talked a head nurse in the hospital into accepting my narcotics count without bothering to re-check it herself; sometimes I conned a pharmacist into adding some extra drugs here and there for "emergencies." Eventually, I stole narcotics, not only from hospital supplies, but from the offices or the bags of other doctors.

By mid-May, even massive doses of Demerol by mouth weren't helping me. One night, after Kay, now expecting Doug in a few weeks, had gone to bed, I went into the kitchen, which was right beside my office, boiled water in a tablespoon, dissolved Demerol tablets in it, sterilized a needle while the solution was cooling, and then shot it intramuscularly. The first time I shot about two hundred milligrams of Demerol, the drug deadened the pain enough for me to get about four hours of uninterrupted sleep, so I thought that the problem might have been licked at last. If I could only get by on four hours' sleep at night for a few more weeks, I figured, I'd be all right, because by then I would be on my way to Ohio and would surely be able to stop shooting. (This is typical junkie thinking: *Just give me a few days, or a few weeks, and I'll be all right; in the meantime, I won't need any more than I'm taking now to keep going.*) However, even after I began shooting Demerol, the relief lasted only a short time. Soon, shots and all, I was back where I had been before—up and down, in and out of bed, shooting a few hundred milligrams here, a few hundred there, and getting virtually no sleep at all.

In accordance with a previous plan, I gave up practically all my Bangor practice in early June to help convert the big old house in Brewer into three apartments, which I had already rented to friends. Despite my constant exhaustion and pain, I managed to get through the days—but the nights were living torture. Just before Doug was born, I measured off a quarter grain of morphine (a normal dose for a person in extreme pain), cooked it in the spoon, and shot it. Once again I found some relief, but now I had graduated to the most addictive legal drug in this country.

Ordinarily, I would have found it harder to obtain morphine than Demerol, but a unique—although horrible— opportunity arose when one of my colleagues suddenly died. This man, a close friend with whom I had often worked and for whom I had always covered in his absence left a large supply of drugs, including Demerol and morphine, much of which had never been accounted for. Since everyone in the medical community around Bangor knew how close we had been, it appeared perfectly natural for me to go to his office to check things out. I dropped over there and appropriated the narcotic supply, which seemed more than enough to get me by until it was time to leave for Ohio. I was thinking, once again, like a typical junkie: *Give me a good supply now, and I can last until the target date, when I know I'll stop.*

If I had continued to take a quarter grain of morphine every three or four hours, I would have had more than enough to last me for the few weeks remaining before we left for Cuyahoga Falls, where we were planning to stay with my parents while waiting for my Cleveland residency to start. But, as usual, I found that this dosage was hardly enough to keep me out of pain. At first, reluctant to increase the dosage, I remained at a quarter grain but shot more often. Then, a week or ten days before we left, I upped my morphine intake to half a grain at a time, tried to cut back to every three or four hours, failed, and soon was taking half grains as often as I had been taking quarter grains before.

By now I needed morphine to get me through the day as well as the night. With Kay around, I had to be careful. I shot when she was resting or doing something in another part of the house, always careful to use the bathroom farthest from wherever she happened to be. However, during the weeks I had been on heavy narcotics, I had no appetite and had to force myself to eating; in the process I lost about thirty pounds, a loss that even a man of my size could not disguise. When Kay began asking what was wrong, I blamed it all on the pain. I got away with that only because she was preoccupied with her approaching confinement. Then, after Doug was born, on June 9, he took up so much of her time that she still didn't suspect anything for a while.

I got all the way up to eight to twelve tablets (two or three grains) of morphine every two hours, then took Nembutal or Seconal (often both) at bedtime in frantically futile attempts to knock myself out. With the morphine keeping me hyperactive all day, the sleeping pills did practically no good at all. On the contrary, half a dozen times a night I was getting up to shoot Demerol. I guess that taking Demerol was a concession to my conscience, if not my training as a doctor—I knew that *nobody* had any business shooting morphine around the clock.

As I looked ahead to the Ohio trip, the prospect of withdrawal became more and more frightening. Never having been through it, I had no real idea of what to expect. I had definitely decided to go off narcotics cold turkey, and to start tapering off on the way to Ohio. When the time finally came, Kay and the baby flew there, while I drove there with Karen (then about three and a half) and her cocker spaniel.

We saw Kay and Doug off at the airport one day and left in the station wagon the next. Despite my fear, I felt I would be all right if I had enough morphine and Demerol to carry me through. I took with me all I had been able to find in the house—about fifteen hundred milligrams of Demerol and fifty quarter-grain tablets of morphine. The Demerol was a recent windfall. Although I had given up my formal practice, I continued to take care of a few imminently terminal cases. In supplying one patient, who could take a hundred milligrams every four hours, with enough to carry him until he died, I had acquired the rest for my own use. The morphine was the last of the supply I had taken from the office of my late doctor friend.

By the time I had the car loaded it was about 11:00 A.M. Even as I left the old mansion in Brewer, I was planning the first stop, an hour and a half to the southwest, for the shot I knew I would need then. I had conned myself into thinking that it (and subsequent shots I would take on the trip) was only to ease the pain in my back and legs.

But deep in my heart I knew better. I was hooked.

II

Drug addicts often con themselves into thinking they can do what they can't do. When I set out for Ohio from Brewer, with Karen beside me on the front seat and the spaniel curled up on the floor in back, I looked forward to an easy, enjoyable trip. Karen and I got along well, and the prospect of being on the road with her for a couple of days pleased me. I was headed for a new life, a new residency, and a year of the kind of work I wanted to do. Both my people and Kay's were close enough to my new place of work for us to see them on weekends, and the new baby would add to their pleasure and ours. There was every reason in the world for my mind to be at ease. I was even unperturbed about the withdrawal that was bound to occur when my drug supply for the trip ran out. I figured that the skimpiness of the supply itself would make withdrawal gradual, even if I went off, cold turkey, after we reached Cuyahoga Falls.

The only real problem I anticipated as we left Brewer was the possible continuation of my back-and-leg distress, but I was prepared for that, too. The pain couldn't be any worse than it had previously been, and, with everything else going for me, I didn't consider it a potential danger or hindrance to my residency. Still, just in case it did become unbearable, Carl Irwin had given me the name of a good neurosurgeon in Akron whom I could call at any time.

My optimistic attitude lasted for about an hour, during which Karen and I talked father-daughter talk: the baby, hunting and fishing, the prospect of living in a new house, her grandparents, the dog, and all the other interests we held in common. Then I began to realize that sitting in one position was causing me pain, and the pain became more acute as we drove along. I began looking for a filling station, where, while the car was being checked, I could go to the men's room and shoot some morphine—strictly, of course, for "medicinal purposes." *I'm just like any other patient,* I thought, *and I'll treat myself as I would another patient. I have pain, I'll take something for it, and the pain will go away.*

But we hit a long stretch of road without any filling stations. The first one we saw was in front of a general store. I passed it by because there was probably no key to the john, and I had to have a key. As the pain got worse, I found it increasingly difficult to carry on my chat with Karen. She was too young to notice my discomfort, but I finally stopped talking altogether as, with sweat beading my forehead and beginning to slide down both sides of my face, my pain and restlessness became almost unbearable.

An hour and a half out of Brewer, we finally reached a regular filling station. I pulled the wagon up to the pumps, told the attendant to fill up the tank, asked Karen if she had to go to the bathroom—she didn't—and then requested the key to the men's room. When the attendant told me it was on a hook inside, I forced myself to remain calm as I got out of the car, found the key, and walked around the side of the station. Once inside the men's room, I locked the door and, suddenly hit by real terror, leaned against it for a minute, thinking the worst of everything. *What if I'm in here too long? What will the attendant think? Does he have another key, as most filling stations do in case one is lost? What if he comes in to investigate and catches me shooting? What if he asks me questions and isn't satisfied with my answers? What if he calls the police?*

Thinking about the possibilities left me limp with fright. Knowing that I had to shoot and get out of there as soon as I could, I turned on the hot water full blast, took my syringe out of one jacket pocket and a couple of morphine tablets out of another, tore the jacket off, and rolled up the left sleeve of my shirt. When the water was hot, I rinsed out the syringe, put in the tablets, watched them dissolve, and, after a last look at the door, shot the morphine. Then I leaned against the sink for a few seconds until I felt better, and, after quickly cleaning the syringe and adjusting my shirt, put on the jacket, unlocked the door, and walked out. By then, I felt pretty good. *Now*, I thought, *I'll be all right. I won't have to shoot for another four hours.*

Of course, I was only kidding myself. I had been shooting something every two hours around the clock for three weeks. In fact, the last thing I had done before leaving the house in Brewer was to shoot morphine, and that had been less than two hours earlier; I would need another shot within two hours. Of course, I wouldn't admit this, not even to myself. *This is a tapering-off trip, a trip to make cold turkey more bearable, isn't it?*

The filling station stop was the first of many. We drove a long way, picking up Route Two to Bennington, Vermont, going through the Cherry Valley in upper New York State. Every hour and a half, I had to stop for shots, several in the afternoon and gathering dusk, while Karen slept beside me on the front seat. We went about five hundred miles that day, more than halfway to Cuyahoga Falls; by the time we checked into a tourist cabin between Syracuse and Buffalo, I was left with four tablets of morphine and beginning to work on the Demerol.

I took Karen across the road to a small restaurant where,

while she ate a full hot meal, I nibbled on a sandwich, most of which I left on the plate. The child, lively, happy, excited, wide awake, didn't seem to notice my lack of appetite. When we went back to our cabin, she asked if I would get her tricycle out of the car. I hadn't had a shot for nearly two hours, and when I reached in for the three-wheeler, I was too shaken up to pull it out. I told Karen to wait a minute and went into the cabin, where I shot eight cc's of Demerol. I stood in the bathroom, leaning against the sink, waiting for relief, but the Demerol had *no* effect. Finally, after ten minutes, I shot the last of the morphine. That worked. Five minutes later, I went out where Karen was patiently waiting, told her where she could ride without being endangered by cars coming into the driveway, and easily pulled her bike out of the back of the wagon. The morphine didn't really give me a lift—only an illusion of stability.

After Karen, who had always been very obedient, began to ride her bike in the areas I had told her were safe, I went into the cabin, took off my shoes, jacket, and tie, and lay down on one of the beds in an attempt to relax. The pain was coming back, and I hoped that complete relaxation would lessen it. Although it was less than half an hour since I had taken the morphine, I would have shot more if there had been any left. I tried not to think about the fact that it was gone, but that kept coming into my mind. Had I followed the schedule I had set for myself before leaving Maine, I would have used up the Demerol first and would have had plenty of morphine now. Instead, all I had was Demerol, and not a great deal of that.

I heard a clap of thunder and saw a flash of lightning through the window. Just as I was struggling up to get Karen inside, she knocked on the door. She was afraid of thunderstorms, and tears were running down her cheeks when I let her in. I cradled her in my arms while she cringed from the storm; that helped me forget my own troubles for fifteen or twenty minutes. When the storm ended, I turned on the television set for her, and while she sat beside me watching, I tried to sleep. Nervous, restless, my back and legs so racked with pain that I couldn't find a comfortable position, I finally got up and took some Seconal. Fifteen minutes later, still on edge and aching, I gave myself a heavy shot of Demerol that knocked me out cold. Fully dressed, I awoke at dawn—not rested, but clearly aware of my surroundings. The first thing I saw was my medical bag on the floor beside the bed—its contents, including pills, needles and other equipment, and medication, scattered on the floor. For a horrified few moments I thought Karen had opened the bag, although she had been trained never to touch it. As she slept beside me, I grabbed her chest, caught a natural heartbeat, felt her breath, shook her, and heaved a long sigh of relief when she woke right up. I let her go back to sleep and then almost in a panic, arose to get some Demerol. Then, for the first time, I noticed a trail of water leading out of the bathroom and extending clear across the room. In the bathroom sink my socks were plugging up the drain. I didn't remember having taken them off, and the only thing I could think of was that Karen, seeing them on the floor, had tried to wash them for me and had left the faucet running.

Suddenly, another wave of terror engulfed me. The place was flooded, yet the tap wasn't on. *Somebody came in and shut it off*, I thought. *My God, who could it have been? Seeing me on the bed with most of my clothes on, he must have known I had knocked myself out. Had he reported me to the police? Or called a doctor? Or told anybody? How could he ignore a fully dressed man asleep on a bed, with pills and syringes and doctor's gear spilled all over the floor while*

water ran from the tap? My back and legs killing me, my
nerve ends tingling, my terror of being discovered becoming
more and more acute, I shot the last of the Demerol. After
waiting a few minutes to pull myself together, I went to the
front office to see if I could find out who had come into the
room and what he had done when he got there. A chunky,
middle-aged man who identified himself as the owner came
over and said, "Doctor, are you all right?"

"Yes, I'm fine."

"I was worried about you," he said. "Last night the pump
was running and woke me around 2:00 A.M. When I went
out to look at it, it was smoking and burning, so I knew some
one had left the water on. I heard it running outside your
door and knocked. Your dog barked, but nobody answered,
so I let myself in with the master key, and turned off the
water. Your bag was open and everything was on the floor. I
couldn't wake you, and I thought about calling the state
police, but I decided to check just a few more times first.
When I went in later, I could see that you and your daughter
were breathing, so I didn't call anyone."

Thank God, I thought. And I said, "I'm sorry to have
caused so much trouble and anxiety. I have been working
very hard, preparing to change my base of operations from
Maine to Ohio. I'm on my way there now with my little girl.
We had been driving all day, and I was so nervous and tired
that I took a couple of sleeping pills. That's why you
couldn't wake me. I guess my daughter tried to wash my
socks and forgot to turn off the tap, and the dog must have
upset the bag. Look," I pulled out two twenty-dollar bills and
handed them to him, "take this. If it's not enough for a new
pump I'll give you more."

"This is fine," he said, accepting the money. "I'm glad I
didn't call anyone. Are you sure you're all right?"

"Oh, yes."

"Well, thanks very much. Sorry I had to go into your cabin. I hope you understand."

"Indeed," I said.

We shook hands, and, badly shaken up, I turned and headed for the cabin. When I got there, Karen was up, dressed and ready to eat. Although I wanted to get out of the place as quickly as possible, I took her to the restaurant across the street and drank black coffee while she had a full breakfast. After we had finished, I managed to get our things together and load the car. Then we drove off, heading west. If all went well, I could make it to Cuyahoga Falls by dinnertime. But all didn't go well. The only thing that I had done according to my original plan since I left Brewer was to *use* up all my drugs. But the supply that I expected to last two days had only lasted one, and now, as I continued to drive and the effects of the Seconal wore off, I became at first slightly nervous, then fearful of what had happened the night before, then, finally, terror-stricken. My legs and back hurt, I had nothing to relieve the pain, and I knew if I didn't get a fix, I wouldn't be able to make it to Ohio.

I didn't. Four hours after leaving the cabin, I told Karen that I was too sick to drive anymore, and we pulled into a motel in Canandagua, New York, hoping that with some sleep, I would be able to go the rest of the way.

I took some Seconal, but that didn't help. Then I took from my bag the empty vials that had contained morphine and Demerol, rinsed out my syringe with hot water, put a couple of cc's of water into each vial, emptied them into the syringe, and shot that—on the chance that there might be a few drops of one of the narcotics left in the vials. There was none. As the unalleviated pain kept getting worse, I realized that I couldn't go any farther without help, so I called my father, told him I was in too much pain to drive, and asked him to come for us.

It was late in the afternoon, Karen's suppertime, and the child was hungry. I managed to take her to the motel restaurant, where she had a good meal. I had nothing, not even coffee, because I was in such agony from my back condition. I expected withdrawal pains in a few hours. I was grateful for one thing, though: back in the room, I had taken enough Seconal and Nembutal to kill a person of normal proportions, but because of my size the drugs only knocked me out.

Meanwhile, although I didn't know it, my parents had left Cuyahoga Falls, some 150 miles to the west, at about 9:00 P.M. Since my father hated to drive at night and made frequent stops for black coffee, he and my mother didn't arrive at the motel until 4:00 A.M. Not wishing to bother us at that hour, they pulled the car over to the side of the road and napped until daybreak. After getting no response when they rapped on our door, which was unlocked, they finally walked in on a shocking scene. Both Karen and I were fully clothed, the little girl fast asleep and I moaning and so unresponsive that when they tried to rouse me, it took nearly half an hour to get me up. In addition to the back pains, withdrawal was beginning, and to this day, I don't know which was worse. All I remember about that morning was my mother starting out in my car with Karen while I rode with my father in his car. Whatever else I know about the trip I later learned from him.

What had horrified my parents most was their discovery of one of my hunting revolvers on the night table beside the bed. I don't remember taking it out of a suitcase, nor why I would want to, unless my pain was so terrible that I thought of killing myself. According to my father, I explained that I wanted to have it handy because I was afraid that someone would break into the room. He said he accepted that explanation because he realized that even talking was painful to me—otherwise, he would have asked why, if I were afraid of anyone breaking in, I had left the door unlocked. Somewhere along the line I volunteered the information that I had taken heavy doses of sleeping pills, which accounted for the difficulty in getting me up. But aside from those few bits of conversation, I did little talking. He told me about meeting Kay and the baby when they got off the plane and how they both seemed fine, but I don't recall either that or anything else he said on the trip. I was too busy concentrating on my misery, frequently changing my position in hopeless attempts to get comfortable and trying vainly to sleep. I didn't even recall stopping at a roadside stand, where we met my mother and Karen to have milk shakes. I can't imagine how I managed to drink mine, because putting anything into my stomach was the last thing on earth I wanted to do. This reluctance to eat, as during active drug addiction, is one characteristic of withdrawal. The very thought of food is nauseating.

We arrived in Cuyahoga Falls in mid-afternoon. I think it was then that Kay, the only adult in the house who had ever seen me this way before, first suspected that I was addicted as well as in pain. She greeted me coldly and barely spoke to me during the two or three days that we subsequently spent in my parents' house before leaving for what was supposed to be a ten-day vacation in Michigan prior to the beginning of my obstetrics residency at the Huron Road Hospital in Cleveland. During the entire period preceding that trip, I was in withdrawal, suffering hellish agony.

While my father spent hours at my bedside, Kay didn't come up to see me once. This might have been partially due to her disgust for my addiction, but it was also a result of Kay's basic personality. She hated to witness any suffering; her reaction was one of panic rather than of pity. This was not entirely her fault, for she had had some psychological problems even before we were married.

I met her in Alliance, her home town, at Mount Union College from which we graduated as classmates in 1943. Five feet seven inches tall, she was an attractive blue-eyed brunette who had majored in English and dramatic speech. We both liked to sing, and much of our mutual attraction had stemmed from our participation in songfests and glee club activities at college. She told me then that she sometimes suffered from unaccountable fears and had sought and received help from a school psychologist, but neither of us considered this serious enough to affect our future happiness together. This, of course, was whistling in the dark, for, although she could be charming, she was subject to extreme changes of mood, a trait she rarely—but occasionally—showed before we were married. Young, in love, about to go overseas, I was confident that I could always pull her through any problems that might come up later.

We were married in Alliance the following October as soon as I received my navy commission. She went with me to Little Creek, Virginia, where I took amphibious training before leaving to participate in several Pacific invasions. When I got out of the service to start medical school, Kay augmented our GI Bill of Rights income by teaching music for a year. With two partners, I opened a medical bookstore which brought in some money, while Kay and I collected more doing both chorus and solo singing. Her talents as a pop singer gained her a thirty-week-a-year minimum contract with Loew's Capital Theater in Washington, D.C., where she sang on stage for three years. I was a bass-baritone—I still have a deep, resonant singing voice—but could also take tenor parts. We got our bookings through Justin Lawrie, a locally well-known musical impresario who handled most of the big government functions. Once we sang at a White House correspondents dinner on President Eisenhower's birthday, attended by such political luminaries as Richard Nixon (then vice-president), Lyndon Johnson (then senate majority leader), and the President of Mexico.

During this period, Kay required professional help to control her recurrent problems, but I still felt that she would be all right once I had my medical degree and went into practice. She had no trouble of any consequence in Maine other than brief, sporadic periods of deep depression. However, the danger of a breakdown was always present, I suppose, and now my own addiction unquestionably helped to bring one on. Kay's lack of either sympathy for me or understanding of my problems eventually developed into open animosity, of which the first real sign came the day I arrived, in such horrible shape, at my parents' home in Cuyahoga Falls.

No matter how much you may read about narcotics withdrawal, or how many times you may see its effects in movies or on television, it is impossible to imagine its agony without going through it yourself. When I left Maine, certain that I could handle whatever might happen to me, I had no idea of what I was bargaining for. In addition to the physical pain of withdrawal, the terror that accompanies it goes beyond the panic state. Every fear, magnified beyond description, builds up until it almost surpasses the nausea, headaches, chest pains, stomach cramps, unbearable fraying of nerve ends, hot waves so intense that you rip off your clothes and want to crawl into a refrigerator, and cold waves so frigid that you bury yourself to no avail in blankets. While going through one physical horror so violent that you can't imagine anything worse, you suddenly are hit by another one ten times as bad. And through it all, for days on end, the panic is always there, devastating your mind while you absorb the agonies of your body. You don't hallucinate, but you can't face anything, not even life itself. It's the sort of panic you might experience when you walk into a room so dark you are enveloped in pitch-blackness: you know there's a light switch, you know where it is, you know where to reach it, you know that all you have to do is snap it—but you can't find it. You reach and reach, but nothing is there, and you stand in that blackness knowing that it's going to stay that way, knowing that you can do nothing about it, knowing that you are blindly helpless and that the blackness will always be there.

That's the way it was for me, there in the home of my parents. I was aware of my father sitting at the edge of the bed, watching me through tear-filled eyes, suffering with me, seeing his tall, powerful son alternately sweating and shivering, his eyes and nose streaming, foam issuing from his mouth as he turned frantically from side to side trying in vain to get comfortable. My father lived through those agonies with me as though he himself were suffering them. Sometimes, he would talk to me in a soft, soothing voice, like a mother crooning to a weeping child, but more often he just watched. He didn't know that I was addicted, only that I was under the influence of something horrible that I was fighting—and he knew it had to be *my* fight, that there was nothing he or anyone else could do to help me. Sometimes I saw him clearly and wanted to cry out for him, sometimes he was just one of many shadows, and sometimes, in my agony, I couldn't see him at all.

My withdrawal reached its peak the second day we were in Cuyahoga Falls. When it was over, although the pain, the temperature changes, and all the other symptoms remained, the panic subsided, and I could talk coherently. Kay had taken the children to her sister's; my father phoned her there and asked if she wanted to take me to a cottage in Travers City in the Michigan woods (it was owned by a woman who worked for the local Board of Education, and she had told my folks that it was available). Kay and I agreed that a week or ten days up there might be able to help us both. While Doug stayed with my parents, we took Karen and the dog, and headed north. It should have been a restful, pleasant ten days, a time of understanding, reconciliation, and recovery. It should have given me all the satisfaction of the streams and woods of Maine I loved so dearly. In short, it should have been a perfect place for me to relax and get ready for my hospital residency in Cleveland, now just a couple of weeks away.

Instead, it was a nightmare. My withdrawal pains were slowly going away, but the less I felt them, the more I felt the really hard pain in my back and legs. I knew the operation in Bangor had not been a success, that I could never be comfortable again without more surgery, that, whether I liked it or not—even if it meant giving up that residency—I would have to put myself back into the hands of a neurosurgeon. As much as I hated to do it, I went to Cleveland after returning to Cuyahoga Falls and told the hospital administrators that I couldn't accept the residency. Then, back in Cuyahoga Falls, I called the Akron doctor whom Carl Irwin had recommended to me when I left Maine. He came right out to see me, and, after ascertaining that the pain was more than I could tolerate, he put both my legs in traction, with weights on pulleys, right there in my parents' house. I wasn't allowed out of the bed, except to go to the bathroom, for six weeks. At the end of those six weeks, the pain was as bad as it had ever been. By then, it was late summer; for the second time in less than a year, I faced back surgery. The only alternative was pain, and I could stand that no longer.

I had kicked the drug habit. As I rode in an ambulance from Cuyahoga Falls to the Garfield Hospital in Akron, I was sure that that, at least, was permanent.

III

THE hospital tests and the fusion operation that followed in Akron were more or less standard procedures for disc patients with a surgical history such as mine. After routine mylograms, I was given an electromyography, which is to the muscles what an electrocardiogram is to the heart. A very large gauge needle is inserted in each muscle whose nerves are damaged. The needle receives an electrical charge from the nerve impulses, and in this way measures the muscle reaction. The number of nerve impulses indicates the extent to which the nerve may still function. Like an electrocardiogram, the electromylogram produces a graph giving the doctors a visual record of the test. My graph showed that I had received more nerve root injury since the first operation, indicating that scar tissue had grown into the sheath of additional nerves, immobilizing them and preventing them from functioning properly. There is some pain involved in an electromyography, although no more than in a mylogram—which is nothing compared to the pains I had been suffering from the injury itself and its complications.

The first operation just hadn't taken, making the second one mandatory. This fusion was of the same two lumbar vertebrae that had been operated upon before, L-3 and L-4. The procedure also included cutting free the affected nerve roots and extracting bone from the right hip for use in the fusion. The operation was performed on October 2, 1954, and I was hospitalized for three weeks afterwards. I went by ambulance from the hospital to my parents' home in Cuyahoga Falls, and was confined to bed until about a week before Christmas.

Nobody in the Garfield Hospital had known that I was addicted. I had never asked for medication, but simply took that which was given to me. This had included Demerol in decreasing amounts after the operation, so that I was weaned away from it just like any other patient. By the time I left the hospital, I was on nothing stronger than Bufferin, and took nothing stronger while convalescing in Cuyahoga Falls. I could tolerate pain and, later, walk, although it soon became apparent to me that my physical capacities were, and would probably continue to be, extremely limited. I now knew that under no circumstances could I ever specialize in obstetrics, which is strenuous and requires a lot of bending. After thinking things over, I decided to take up anesthesiology, a field that had always interested me as it seemed to require quick thinking rather than physical endeavor. I called Dr. Clem Dwyer, head of the anesthesiology department at the Eastern Maine General Hospital in Bangor, and he agreed to let me begin a two-year residency there in mid-January, 1955.

Although I continued to have pain during the few weeks that elapsed between leaving Cuyahoga Falls and starting the Bangor residency, I never thought it would become intense enough to stand in the way of my appointment. I didn't expect to be entirely free from pain (I haven't been to this day), but I hardly anticipated that the pain would become intolerable. Nevertheless, it grew steadily worse and, for the first time since my trip with Karen, I was acutely reminded of the relief that I had received from narcotics. Every intensification of pain brought an intensification of desire.

It is no myth that drug addicts and alcoholics can never be cured. I am today a *nonusing addict* and a *nondrinking alcoholic*, and my only guarantee that I won't resume either habit is my own strength of will, the result of the determination to live from one day to the next rather than to worry about the future or indulge in self-condemnation for the past. In those days just before returning to Maine from Ohio, I had two things going for me: the still vivid memory of the terrors of withdrawal, and that I had been through only one relatively brief sustained bout with narcotics.

But, like every other addict, I had never completely lost my sense of need for drugs. Most of the time, I could hide the feeling somewhere in the back of my mind, keeping it under control by telling myself repeatedly that I would never take drugs again. Sometimes I couldn't make that desire for a shot go away that easily; the need was there, plain and sure, yet fortunately not so intense that I could not spar with it and overcome it. Occasionally, however, it became so acute that it took more than mere sparring to drive it off. I had to make a Herculean effort to fight it, especially when my physical discomfort was almost more than I could bear. During that period, I won every fight until, back in Maine, I was certain that I had kicked the habit for good. Because of the pain, I flew to Bangor with Kay and the children, while my father drove my car, a new one I had acquired in Akron. The pain persisted, but I reported on schedule to Dr. Dwyer at the Eastern Maine General. Although I had a full-time residency, the hours were not too tiring and, since I lived so close to the hospital—we had taken over the first-floor apartment of our big old house in Brewer—it was easy to get to and from work. I looked forward to an enjoyable two years among men whom I knew well, doing the work I wanted to do, under a fine, considerate chief.

But my back pains knocked out everything. I lasted only

four days in the residency before I had to call on Dr. George Wood, an internist and close friend, for help. He put me to bed, where I stayed most of the time for nearly a year, from January to November, 1955. Except for the birth of our third child, Dana, on October 29, the entire year was a dead loss. Everything in my life revolved around the harrowing, incessant pain. Here and there came a few short periods of relief, but they were measured in minutes and hours, not days and weeks. Not a day passed for me without suffering hard pain for some length of time. While I couldn't have eliminated it, I could have temporarily alleviated it with narcotics, but I didn't dare.

George Wood, one of the most understanding men I have ever known, must have realized why I never asked for any, although I never told him that I had been addicted. During those long months, we talked about all manner of subjects, from sports to music, from hunting to philosophy, from professional discussions of my condition to conversations about the marvelous machinery of the human body and its ability to absorb punishment. We talked about drugs, too. Although neither of us directly mentioned my addiction, we often spoke in general terms of the dangers of addiction when pain is so great that narcotics seem to provide the only relief. We weren't kidding each other. George had to know I was an addict because I kept repeating my fear of addiction. I was sure that he knew, because he was too perceptive to be fooled. Yet he never directly suggested that I was knowingly addicted. He simply accepted my explanation that I refrained from requesting drugs because I feared addiction. My desire was intense, but I thought that I could lessen it by talking about it, and, in fact, that did help.

As busy as he was, he rarely missed a day at my home; sometimes, if he saw a light in my window on his way back from a house call, he came at two or three in the morning. When I heard his car pull into the driveway, I managed to struggle out of bed and meet him in another room so we wouldn't bother Kay, who was pregnant with Dana. George might stay for ten or fifteen minutes, or for an hour or more. He was doctor, friend, confidante, philosopher, and sometimes even spiritual adviser. It was his kindness and encouragement that pulled me through those months of agony without narcotics.

Another man who helped me was my next-door neighbor, Reed Davis. A daily visitor, he had a classic "down-east" sense of humor, funny not for *what* is said, but *how* he said it. Whenever *I* try to repeat one of Reed's lines that broke me up at the time, it comes out flat. You had to see *him* to appreciate his wisecracks. The look on his face, the Maine accent, the sardonic smile, transformed an ordinary remark or gesture into a real belly laugh.

One day he came over with a big package, which he showed me before taking into the kitchen.

"What is it?" I said.

"A nine-pound-two-ounce pork roast," he said.

Before I could thank him—for he knew that I liked pork—he added, "My brother sent it to me. He owns a market. But my family ain't big enough to eat that much meat. I'm giving it to you so it won't spoil."

Just as he was leaving, Kay, obviously pregnant, looked into the bedroom to thank him for the roast. After she left he said, "Your back and legs ain't so good, but there's nothing wrong with the rest of you. Why didn't you holler, 'Rape'?"

Instead of subsiding with bed rest, the pain became so bad that I could stand it no longer, and I finally asked George for a shot of Demerol. He gave me a normal dose of seventy-five or a hundred milligrams, then said, "Jim, you can't go on this way. You need more help than I can give you."

"Surgery," I mumbled. I had been dreading it all year, but knew that it had to come.

"Whom do you want?"

"Joe Barr," I said.

"I'll call him."

Dr. Joe Barr, who died four or five years ago, was a world-famous orthopedic surgeon who was on the staff of the Massachusetts General Hospital in Boston. George Wood phoned him, and a few days later, after Joe had studied my X rays, made an appointment with him for me about two weeks later. George gave me a normal shot of Demerol every day while I waited to go to Boston, and it did help to ease the pain. Although tempted, I refrained from shooting the stuff myself. It was safer to let George do it. When the two weeks were up, I almost believed I wasn't addicted, after all. *Almost.* I had been clean for over a year, but not from lack of desire. The desire, although dormant most of the time, was always present, always ready to rise to the surface, a formidable opponent with which I would always have to cope.

The trip from Brewer to Boston was very rough—by ambulance to the Bangor railroad station, about six hours by train to Boston, then by ambulance to the Massachusetts General Hospital. Kay went with me, but I made her go right home because the 1955 polio epidemic in Boston was still in its final stage. Besides, we were both concerned about the new baby and the two older children, all of whom needed their mother.

Joe Barr and two other old doctor friends of mine, Bill Sweet and Tom Delorme, worked on me preoperatively, repeatedly taking mylograms and administering Demerol and morphine to ease my pain before deciding to go ahead with surgery. I took the medication without comment or protest. They didn't know that I was addicted, and I didn't tell them.

The operation, my third in two years, was extremely complicated. Barr, with Sweet assisting, had to cut away the nerve root that had adhered from the previous surgery, tear out the previous fusion (which, instead of fusing, had just laid down a bonelike calcium deposit), and take bone from my hips to fuse all five lumbar vertebrae. Joe Barr was particularly good at this type of intense fusion, which, even when successful, is never permanently painless. (Today, more than fifteen years later, I am usually in some pain and occasionally have periods bad enough to drive me into bed for a few days. I have had to learn to live with it, since it will last as long as I do.)

Following the operation, I was put into a tailor-made corset-type steel brace from spine-end to shoulders with six or seven individual bars conforming to the curvature of my body; from the day it was fitted on me at the hospital, I wore it day and night for about eight months. If all went according to schedule, I would be in the hospital from four to six weeks. I never asked for the exact date of my release, fearing it would be put off a little longer, and I was thoroughly fed up with being a hospital patient instead of a doctor.

I was taken off drugs post-operatively in a routine manner and with no difficulty. The procedure was quite familiar to me—cutting down the dosage of narcotics after the first five or six days until it was eliminated altogether. Because of my size, I was getting a bit more than the average person, starting with 200 milligrams of Demerol every four hours. This was cut in half, then cut in half again to 50 milligrams, and finally changed from shots to capsules of Demerol, and, later, to codeine. There were days when I had a desire for heavier doses, but I could control that easily enough. By then, I was more interested in getting out of the hospital in time to pick up my anesthesiology residence again in February, 1956, than in the possible effect of narcotics upon me.

Five weeks after the operation, I summoned up enough courage to ask Joe when I was going home.

"Next Wednesday," he said.

"Wonderful," I exclaimed.

On Tuesday, he came by and asked, "How are you going there, Jim?"

"By air."

He shook his head. "You can't sit long enough to fly to Maine."

"I've been walking. How much time before I *can* sit that long?"

"Maybe four weeks."

"The hell with that," I said. "What if I got somebody to take me up on a stretcher?"

"That would be all right."

After phoning Northeast Airlines, the only commercial line that went to Bangor, and learning that it couldn't fly stretcher cases, I got in touch with Dr. Don Bridges, an obstetrician in Bangor and a good friend of mine who knew somebody in the Air Force Reserve, and would ask if he could arrange something. He phoned back twenty minutes later, to tell me that there were plenty of reserve officers in his outfit who had to put in flight time every month and would be glad to come to Boston for me. We agreed to meet at noon the following day at Boston's Logan Airport, and Joe Barr got an ambulance to take me there. At the airport two officers, a colonel and a major, came down from Bangor with Don in a C-47, complete with a stretcher. They helped me walk up the stairs to the plane, and we had a pleasant flight of about an hour and a half, staying high enough to keep out of turbulence. It was a sunny December day, with a cloudless sky and the Atlantic glistening smooth as glass on the right as I looked out the window. At the Bangor end, Kay met me with an ambulance, so that the only other time I had to move was to get down the steps from the plane.

The next three or four weeks, although painful, were satisfying. I couldn't move around much, but I was with my family and looking forward to my long-delayed residency under Clem Dwyer at the Eastern Maine General. My only problem—and it scared me—was the pain. I didn't expect miracles, but I thought it would lessen as I became stronger. It didn't. Looking back, I realize that it wasn't much worse than it is today, but it bothered me enough to let the old temptation and desire for relief grow as the weeks went on.

Clem told me not to rush things; that if I found I couldn't report exactly on February 1, he would hold the residency for me. He also helped arrange a physiotherapy course of treatment and massage, to be given at noon every day by a hospital therapist, Steve Merriweather, in accordance with Joe Barr's recommendations. Although grateful for everything that everyone had done and was willing to do for me, I still had that nagging pain, and, even worse, an increasing desire for a shot.

One shot, I thought. *What possible harm can it do after all I've been through? I'm not addicted. If I were, I would have started long ago. I shouldn't have this pain after that big operation. It should be going away. I know I'll always have a little pain, but it shouldn't be this bad. One small shot. It could make all the difference.* I rationalized: *They gave it to me in the hospital and they got me off just the way they get everyone off. It didn't have any unusual effect on me. The pain. I've had so much for so long. A few hours' relief—that's all I need. And one shot will give me that. Just one. Then I won't ever take any more.*

It was dangerous thinking—typical junkie thinking—and I

knew it. During the previous year I had endured worse pain
for longer periods, yet had managed to accept drugs only
under strict control with another person administering them.
I couldn't tell you today why I needed a fix so badly at that
particular time. All I know is that I did, and that, somehow
or other, I had to get one.

I spent the first three months of my residency as an
observer because I didn't have the strength to do the work. I
had seen many operations, of course, but my concentration
had always been up, on the surgical process; now, I watched
the anesthesiologist. Normally, such observation time is not
considered part of a residency, but, thanks to Clem Dwyer
and two members of his staff, it counted as credit toward my
program.

After spending most of my first morning of residency in
the operating room, I went home to rest because, I told
myself, I wanted to go back to the hospital that night to see
preoperative patients and to watch one of the staff men
check conditions for anesthesia. This was only partly true.
My real reason was to take that one shot that I had had in
mind for so long, and throughout the afternoon I thought of
nothing else. The pain had not diminished—in fact, during the
last two operations that I watched I had to sit down or I
couldn't have tolerated it. I purposely waited until the evening when, with not as much activity going on at the hospital, it was less likely that I would be missed if I disappeared
for a few minutes. Besides, the key to the narcotics box was
in the operating room, and during the day I couldn't possibly
have gotten away with using it for my own purposes.

In the early part of the evening, I tried—and apparently
succeeded, since no one ever mentioned it to me—to hide my
anxiety by asking questions about specific patients and
appearing to concentrate on the answers. Actually, I neither

heard nor understood them, because my desire for a shot had become so obsessive that nothing else mattered. As soon as possible, less than an hour after we had begun to make the rounds, I pleaded fatigue, an easy cop-out for me since I really was tired. But before going home, I sneaked up to the operating room, took the key to the narcotics box, and drew up 1 cc (a quarter grain) of morphine into a syringe. Then, my hand shaking and perspiration pouring down my face, I went into the doctors' dressing room and gave myself an intramuscular shot.

For perhaps fifteen seconds I simply leaned against the door, my mind in a turmoil of shame and terror, my whole body bathed in sweat. Shaking all over, I forgot where I was, why I was there, what I was doing—everything except remorse for having committed a crime against myself by breaking a resolution I had kept for so long. Then, to my horror, the syringe fell out of my quivering right hand and smashed into pieces on the tile floor, bringing me back to reality. Overcome with fear that someone might walk in and surprise me, I got down on my knees and began throwing the remains of the syringe into the toilet. After flushing it, I ran the flat of my hands along every square inch of the floor. In five minutes—possibly less—all vestiges of evidence had literally gone down the drain. To make sure, I stayed on my hands and knees feeling for anything that might be left, but I had done a thorough job, and when I rose to my feet there was no trace of the syringe.

I still had to get out of there, check the narcotics box to make sure it was locked, and return the key to its place in the operating room. But, for another few moments, I couldn't move. Again, I leaned against the door, now breathing heavily and, for the first time, aware that the pain was receding. Soon it would be gone, but I knew that the relief would last only a few hours and then the pain would return to plague me again.

My God, I thought, *what have I done? And where will it lead me?*

Although the pain was becoming more bearable with the passing of the minutes, I gained no satisfaction from the physical comfort that would soon follow, for of all the kaleidoscopic emotions that shook me during the short time I was in the doctors' room, the dominant one was fear—fear of being discovered, fear of being hooked, fear of the future, fear of the true meaning of what I had just done. If I had ever talked myself into thinking I might not be addicted, I had proved once and for all how wrong I had been. I *was* a drug addict. I would always be a drug addict. I would be fighting it as long as I lived. For a long time I had been winning; this time I had lost.

But the moment I straightened up and opened the door a crack to be sure no one was around when I walked out, I felt a glimmer of encouragement. *I can still fight back.* Aloud, I said, "No more. No more."

And for over two years there was no more. Throughout the remainder of my anesthesiology residence, I neither shot nor swallowed a single milligram of narcotics.

IV

Because of my 1955 disability it took me three years to do a two-year residency in Bangor. Anesthesiology was so wide-open at the time that a trained anesthesiologist could almost write his own ticket. The opportunity that looked best to me was at a new hospital in Ellsworth, about twenty miles southeast of Bangor and on the road to Bar Harbor, where the Mt. Desert Hospital, with an excellent staff and good facilities, was easily accessible. The location also offered opportunities for private practice in anesthesiology, which, incidentally, is a field that, contrary to popular opinion, is not confined to administering anesthesia in an operating room. A trained anesthetist must have a thorough knowledge of the patient's medical history, the type of anesthesia he can tolerate (if any), his age, general physical condition, and a dozen other factors. Often, it is the anesthesiologist rather than the surgeon who must make the final decision as to whether it is safe to operate.

Both Kay and I loved the Ellsworth area, which was a rare combination of woods and seashore. We sold the house in Brewer and bought some magnificent property in Lamoine, a tiny community two miles from Ellsworth and about a dozen miles from Bar Harbor. In addition to a huge old mansion that had once been a farmhouse and had been used as a summer home by the previous owners, the property included twelve acres of wood land and a thousand feet of beachfront on Frenchman's Bay. After buying the place from the former owner's widow, Kay and I had a monumental remodeling job done on it. We tore down walls, rearranged rooms, installed a heating system for year-round use, and made other practical and esthetic changes. When we were through, we had a lovely eight-room home in the shape of a square "U", with a twelve-by-twenty-foot living room on one end and a small office on the other. The most striking feature of the living room was a five-by-ten-foot picture window overlooking a big lawn, some neighbors' lobster shacks, and the bay itself, topped off by Cadillac Mountain on Mt. Desert Island across the water. We also designed a big fireplace, a flagstone patio with a stone wall in front of it, and an outdoor grill. The kitchen, laundry, and dining room were in the center of the "U", the bedrooms and baths on the second floor.

It should have been a perfect setup, and I looked forward to a long, productive life there, in one of America's most beautiful settings. However, there were two serious situations which changed this bucolic dream into a nightmare. One was the condition of my back, for the pain there and in my legs was beginning to increase just before we left Brewer; the other was a power struggle in the new Ellsworth Hospital, a political controversy that made it impossible for a staff member to remain neutral. In healthier days, I'm sure I could have handled that—I had never run away from a fight before my illness—but I couldn't tolerate the pain and the hospital tension at the same time. The physical strain on the one hand and the mental strain on the other was a combination that could lead me nowhere but to disaster. And the work load I assumed, beginning almost from the day we set up house-keeping in Lamoine, was far beyond my physical capacities. I think I must have been the only trained anesthetist in the area, because constant calls from Bar Harbor, Ellsworth, and sometimes even Bucksport had me driving 40 or 50 miles a day. My day began at 6:00 A.M. and often didn't end until 2:00 the next morning if there were any emergencies.

When one mistake can cost a life, even a doctor sound in mind and body can feel the pressure. That pressure hit me faster than the average person, and I was a bundle of nerves within weeks. My wife and friends tried to slow me down, but I neither would nor could. A man of my size, in the prime of his life, the mid-thirties, could too easily be accused of faking, and I couldn't stand that. I later learned that this is a fear that haunts almost everyone suffering chronic pain, especially when there is nothing visibly wrong. I looked strong and healthy, and in a new locale where only a few close medical friends knew my condition, there seemed no excuse for me to suffer anything but exhaustion from long hours and demanding work.

Except for the lapse in the doctors' room at the Eastern General in Bangor, I had been drug-free for about three years. Now suddenly, while driving home from Bar Harbor one night, I had that uncontrollable urge again. My pain was intense, my nerves were frayed. I pulled up to the side of the road almost in sight of my house, opened my bag, measured out 50 milligrams of Demerol, heated it, sterilized a syringe with my cigarette lighter, and gave myself a shot. This time there was no fear, no remorse, no self-pity, no regret—only blessed relief. As usual, in order not to wake Kay or the children, I put my car lights out before turning into my driveway, and carefully closed the door before going into the house. I stood for a minute at the foot of the stairs feeling the pain recede, and slowly went up to the bedroom. With Kay asleep, I undressed, washed, and put on my pajamas in the dark, then slid quietly into the bed beside her. Only there did I feel anything akin to remorse, for just before going to sleep, I remember thinking, *What's so good about this?* Indeed, there was nothing good about it, because it started me on a new cycle of drug-taking which snowballed with frightening speed.

My attempt to fight off addiction lasted for a short period —a matter of days—when I tried to settle for codeine, which I took by mouth. But, besides nauseating me, it did nothing for the pain, and I was soon back on Demerol. At first I shot only 50 milligrams of it once every twenty-fours, but it wasn't too long before I needed it every three or four hours or as often as I could get it, and soon I was up to 10 cc's (400 to 500 milligrams) every couple of hours when I could get that much. Then suddenly—and so automatically that I was hardly aware of the change—I began taking morphine, again starting with a small dosage and quickly increasing it.

In the meantime, I hired a driver for five dollars a day—my next-door neighbor who, although disabled with rheumatoid arthritis, was able to take me back and forth between Ellsworth and Bar Harbor and occasionally to Bucksport. This eliminated a little of the work pressure, but that worry had long since been replaced by anxiety about drugs. In the meantime, the political problem at the Ellsworth Hospital became so acute that, with two groups of people trying to cut each other's throats, there was hardly time for patients. I continued as a member of the staff, but I had so little to do there that almost all of my attention was concentrated on cases at Bar Harbor.

As the weeks passed, I began doing what every junkie does—feigning normalcy while using every possible device to wangle narcotics wherever they might be obtained. Because of the turmoil at the Ellsworth Hospital, I did more con jobs there than in Bar Harbor, where the business of treating patients was carried on without regard for internal politics. I convinced my doctor friends in Ellsworth first to give me occasional shots and later to write prescriptions for me. I would often have a doctor give me a prescription for 30 cc's of Demerol, which I could cross out and change to 20 cc's of morphine. I wrote phony prescriptions for my own patients, always for morphine, because Demerol was soon giving me no relief at all. Being a pretty good faker, I managed to make everything appear on the up-and-up, and even fooled Kay completely. (She was pregnant with Julie, our fourth child and second daughter, who was born in December, 1958.) When I felt any remorse at all, it was for my neglect of the children. I had neither the time nor the inclination to take Karen or the boys hunting in the woods, and this bothered my conscience more than anything.

Of course, this was not the only thing about which I should have been conscience-stricken, for I now thought nothing of stealing drugs from other doctors and making switches that could endanger patients.

Concentrating almost exclusively on the Ellsworth hospital, I went from doctor to doctor for prescriptions, getting them filled in as many different drug stores as I could find. More and more often, I went to the hospital at night, where one nurse-anesthetist assisted me whenever I took part in an operation. We kept all our drugs in an anesthesia box, including curare, Demerol, and morphine. With me there, she didn't bother to keep track of what we had except to check the chart, which I made up myself. I started replacing the drugs with sterile water, conning myself into thinking that there was no way this could make a difference to patients. Actually, while doing the patient no harm organically, this replacement could prolong discomfort, since sterile water, of course, is no pain-killer. There were no mistakes when I was there, because I knew which vials contained drugs and which water, but if an emergency arose in my absence it would be possible for a patient in pain to be given water instead of the drug he was supposed to get. Fortunately for me (and my conscience) this was highly unlikely, and, to the best of my knowledge, it never happened.

In the early days of my switching, I wasn't concerned about getting caught because, even though the drug nurses checked the count when they changed shifts, they had no way of knowing about my activities. The drugs I took looked just like water. As long as the vials were filled, nothing in the narcotics box appeared to be missing. Sometimes I drained the entire supply of narcotics in the anesthesia box, but I salved my conscience and conned myself by giving a suffering patient atropine or scopolamine, which are often administered to people on anesthesia anyway. These drugs reduce stomach, bowel and vocal cord spasms by drying up secretions that might otherwise cause vomiting or even strangulation. I could easily rationalize the administration of these drugs to my patients, since I had taken them prior to my own surgery at the Massachusetts General, and they are used in many other hospitals for the same purpose. While this was junkie reasoning, it carried enough justification to eliminate any fear I might otherwise have had of harming patients.

Everything—the purchase and remodeling of the house, and ballooning of my practice, my re-addiction, and eventually my own realization that even with drugs my pain was more than I could stand—happened within a period of about three months. By then, having dropped 35 or 40 pounds because I couldn't eat, I was in worse shape than I had been before. Because I had to stay in bed much of the time, my practice collapsed as quickly as I had built it, and we all knew that something had to be done. I'm not sure whether Kay had suspected my addiction. I kept telling her my weight loss and the weakness that went with it were caused by the pain, which was really partly true—in fact, I could easily convince myself that it was entirely true, since the pain led to the addiction, as it had before.

Sometimes I tried fighting off the addiction by starting into withdrawal, but I couldn't make it last. I might go for a couple of days before falling back into the same old trap, but it was impossible to get beyond the early stages. My only successful withdrawal at that point had come on our "vacation" trip to Michigan, and when I thought of the horrors of that experience, my desire for a fix overcame everything else. I was on a vicious merry-go-round, conning, stealing, shooting, until, unable to stand the pressure or overcome the fears of detection and the attacks of conscience, I tried withdrawing. When that didn't work, back I went to satisfy my hunger for drugs, a hunger I used my pain to justify but I knew better, as I had known better on the trip to Ohio with Karen. I was so strung out on narcotics that, however intense the pain, the desire for drugs was greater.

One day, while I was in one of those early withdrawal stages, a car drove up in front of the house and two men got out and came to the door. Both were friendly, quiet, well-dressed, and extremely polite. The older one, about fifty-five, of average height and weight, wore glasses. The younger one, was a tall, well-built, nice-looking fellow in his early thirties. Both could have been important businessmen, and, as I went to answer the door, I wondered what they wanted.

"I came from Boston to see you," the older one said. He pulled out an identification card as he added, "I'm an FBI investigator. This gentleman is a Maine State narcotics agent. We'd like to ask you a few questions. Do you mind if we come in?"

I froze, yet managed to toss off what seemed to me a

perfectly normal, firmly voiced "Not at all. Just follow me."

I took them through the living room, where Kay was sitting quietly while the children played. As I walked, carefully trying not to stumble, thoughts of total disaster ran through my confused mind: *They've caught up with me. It had to come. I wonder if they'll take me away. How did they know? Who told them? What can I say? Am I going to jail? They've got to let me stay home. They can't do this to me in front of my wife and children. They've got to give me a break.*

Like a drunken man suddenly doused with ice water, my mind cleared somewhat as we approached the back room. Withdrawal symptoms, which had plagued me for two days, disappeared in the stress of the moment as I tried to anticipate their questions and frame my answers.

If they know too much, I thought, *nothing that I say will do any good. But how much do they know? I can handle this if I use my head. I've got to be careful. Let them talk. Answer their questions. Don't volunteer anything. And if there's an opening, try to get them onto another subject. They both must know all about guns. I'll show them my collection. And the young guy from Maine must love hunting and fishing. I'll talk about that. Tell them what I can. Cooperate, yet hold back. Please, God, don't let them take me away.*

They followed me into my little office and, after we sat down, one said, "Dr. DeWitt, we've been told that you have been receiving inordinately large amounts of narcotics from local druggists by prescription."

"That's right," I said. "I had a severe back injury a few years ago and often am in great pain. I do need a lot of narcotics, but I get them by legitimate means."

"Are you taking much?"

"Quite a bit, at times."

"How much?"

Careful, Jim, I thought. *It can't be too much or too little.*

"It depends upon the pain," I said. "Sometimes I can get by on 100 milligrams of Demerol a couple of times in a twenty-four-hour period. Sometimes, I need it more often."

"And morphine?"

"I have to take it when the Demerol doesn't stop the pain."

"Do you give it to yourself?"

"Yes," I said. "There's no point in bothering anyone else. I know what to do and how much to take."

"You must take more morphine than Demerol."

Another warning bell sounded in my brain and I thought: *These guys know how much I've been getting by prescription. It's easy enough to check. An agent can cover the whole state in less than half an hour by calling one pharmacist, asking him to call others in his area, and having him call back with a complete list within range of his telephone.*

"I have some very bad days," I said.

"Doctor," said one of the agents, "do you ever get Demerol or morphine for your own use from the anesthesia box at the Ellsworth Hospital?"

My God, I thought, *somebody from the hospital must have called these guys in. It could have been anybody on the opposite side of the fence from me. I have plenty of enemies on the staff. We all do.*

"Never," I said.

"A bottle of Demerol from the anesthesia box was sent to the company that supplied it for analysis," said the older man. "It had been replaced with sterile water. As the staff anesthetist, wouldn't you have charge of some narcotics?"

"Yes," I said. "But I never replaced Demerol or anything else there with sterile water. There's been a political struggle going on at that hospital ever since it was built. I'm sure one of the doctors on the other side staged this in order to hurt me—maybe even get me fired."

They were aware of the hospital's political problems, and we talked about them for a while. Then I got them on the subject of guns and hunting. I showed them my gun rack, explaining that because of my physical condition I had had to turn in most of my rifles for pistols. There weren't any federal gun controls at that time, and I had bought several .45 caliber revolvers from the New York State Police when they shifted to .37 magnums. I also showed them a long-barreled .45 Colt that I had picked up from a magazine ad for thirty-five dollars. I could shoot it accurately enough to hit a deer at fifty or seventy-five yards.

They showed me their guns, either .32 or .38 specials with short barrels, which they carried in shoulder holsters.

"You can't shoot accurately very far with those," I said.

"We don't have to," the Boston man said. "We've had four or five agents killed this year, and they were all hit within distances of eleven feet or less. There's no necessity for us to carry long-range guns."

An hour after they arrived, the two men got up to leave. Both shook hands with me, told me how much they enjoyed the visit, and thanked me for answering their questions. When I took them to the door, they left without mentioning narcotics again. It was, apparently, a routine investigation, with everything left up in the air.

From the window I watched them walk to their car, get in, and drive away. It was an unmarked gray Ford sedan. For years after that, I got a quick chill in my belly every time I saw a gray Ford sedan. Junkies and drunks call the feeling the "cop horrors." I have had it hundreds of times.

That was the first.

V

My first reactions after the agents left were fear of arrest and resentment against whoever had turned me in. That afternoon I went into Ellsworth to see a lawyer, whom I had met through his brother, a surgeon. I told him the same thing I had told the agents, and that I had reason to believe a political enemy on the hospital staff had turned me in. At that time either theft or sale of narcotics were the only actual crimes for which agents or the police might be called upon. Since I had never sold narcotics, the only possible charge against me could be theft. I was guilty of that, but didn't tell the lawyer. All I said was that I doubted that anyone could prove I had stolen drugs, either from other doctors or from the hospital. When he asked if I had access to drugs, I told him about the anesthesia box and that some of the narcotics in it had been taken and replaced with water. The manufacturers had proved this in their own tests, but there was no way of proving who had done it.

He didn't ask me whether I was guilty or not, but said, "Does anyone else have a key to the anesthesia narcotics box?"

"The nurse under me has a key," I said, "and so has the hospital superintendent."

"There are two other keys," he said. "As the anesthetist

you have every right to handle those bottles, so your finger-prints on them don't mean anything. As long as somebody else has keys to the box, there's not much chance of establishing proof that you're the one who replaced the narcotics."

His words reassured me a little, but that didn't help much since I knew I was guilty. On the way home, I made a solemn vow that when I got through with this withdrawal I'd never touch narcotics again. Actually, the day's events had just about scared my withdrawal symptoms away. Although I took no more shots, I got through the next few days so well that withdrawal was nearly complete.

Less than a week after the agents' visit, I was called before the hospital brass, including the chairman of the board of trustees, the chief of medicine, the medical director, and the chief surgeon. I was friendly with the surgeon on a professional level, for we had often worked together on operations, but he was on the other side of the fence in the political battle, which was still going strong. The first thing that was revealed during the meeting was that the surgeon had reported me. The chairman of the board later handed me a paper that he told me to sign. It was my resignation from the staff because of the "general knowledge" that I was overusing narcotics. In my own defense, I pointed out that the surgeon himself had written prescriptions for me, then had reported me to the agents for doing something that he couldn't prove. This, of course, was mere evasion because I *was* guilty of the charges mentioned in the resignation, but I was too upset by the surgeon's action to give up without at least the semblance of a fight. I looked at the surgeon as I talked, but he kept his head down. After a few minutes of pondering following my speech, I realized I had no choice, and signed the resignation.

There were tears of anger welling up in my eyes as I

walked out, and I was determined to speak to the surgeon before leaving the hospital. Knowing that he had to go into the doctor's room for his coat and hat, I went in there to wait for him. When he arrived, I said, "Well, you got what you wanted, didn't you? The least you could have done was to talk to me first."

"It was too bad that this had to happen," he said. "But you shouldn't be taking care of patients."

"If you treat patients the way you treated me, you have less right to be on this staff than I. And, believe me, I'm a patient. You may know enough about the human body to cut it up, but you have no understanding of pain or of the use of drugs to alleviate it. If you had anything to say, you should have said it to me."

The more I talked, the angrier I became, lacing everything I said with curses while the surgeon simply stood there and took it. If I hadn't been disabled, I would have thrown a few punches. It was just as well that I couldn't; I towered over him by about six inches and might have killed the guy.

My anger was not completely unjustified. He should have spoken to me before going to the authorities. I think he may even have sensed that he was wrong, because he made no attempt to defend himself. He knew his action hadn't been guided by sound medical practice or philosophy, but by political animosity. Before I became addicted, I once had to commit an alcoholic doctor with suicidal tendencies to an institution near Bangor, but waited until I could talk to him before going ahead. I think this should be the first therapeutic move in treating a victim of any sort of addiction. Fear of the authorities is an integral part of his problem. Although actually sick, he is filled with remorse and self-pity; arrest, commitment, or the threat of either simply intensifies these feelings. Professional courtesy, while not as important, was another factor that my colleague had ignored, as I pointed out to him with profane vehemence.

Still sick with anger and shame, I finally left the hospital and drove home with tears streaming down my cheeks. I toyed with the idea of telling Kay the truth, but she was well along with Julie and I didn't want to make things any tougher for her than they already were. When I arrived, I didn't have to say much. The minute she saw my red-rimmed eyes and the hangdog look on my face she knew that something had happened. When I told her I resigned under the pressure of the political situation at the hospital I thought that she might come to my arms and try to lend some much-needed comfort. Instead she looked at me in disgust, then turned and walked away, the first indication she suspected my re-addiction. She never had been sympathetic, nor had she ever understood that I was a sick man, not a bad one. To her, addiction was a crime.

Sorely in need of help from someone who *would* understand, I called Dr. Joe Barr in Boston, and we made an appointment for later in the week. At that time, besides giving me the benefit of his human wisdom, which was profound, he could examine me and perhaps find a more sensible cure for my ills than I had tried myself. I had serious doubts about having another operation, if indeed one was possible. Once you undergo the type of multiple fusion I had had, any further surgery might do more harm than good.

When I went to keep my appointment, Joe made it easier for me by telling me that he knew about my addiction. Someone had phoned him from the Ellsworth Hospital to ask about my postoperative drug withdrawal. He had checked the records, found nothing unusual and told the caller my withdrawal course had been entirely normal. When I spoke of my resignation, he said, "I wish you had called me, Jim. I didn't realize what pressure you were under up there, and I might have been able to help you."

As he examined me, he continued to speak in gentle tones about all my problems, physical and psychological. There was nothing he could do to help me physically. My condition would be ameliorated only by time, when the nerve roots would eventually be rechanneled through the scar tissue. This couldn't be done surgically because of the chance that the instruments might hit the motor pathways and cause bowel and bladder paralysis without stopping the pain. I'd just have to sweat it out and let nature take its course.

When I asked him how I could continue to practice in an area where everybody knew that my addiction was so bad that I had been fired, he reminded me that I still had my work to do in Bar Harbor and other places besides Ellsworth.

"They don't want me in Bar Harbor," I said.

"How do you know?"

"After what happened in Ellsworth?"

"Well, let's find out."

He picked up the phone, called the director of the Mt. Desert Island Hospital and asked if he still wanted me. I didn't hear the other end of the conversation, but when Joe hung up, he smiled and said, "They want you, all right! They know what you've been through in Ellsworth and they understand what happened and why. Now, if I were you, I'd go off somewhere for a couple of weeks—maybe to Florida, where you can sit in the sun and forget your troubles."

I thanked him, went home, called my father to borrow about fifteen hundred dollars, and we all flew to St. Petersburg, checking in at one of the beach hotels. It turned out to be a ghastly, almost a disastrous move, because, trapped in one little suite while rain poured down day after day, I felt worse and worse. Eventually, racked with pain, I dragged myself into the bathroom one afternoon and shot some Demerol. When that didn't help, I went to a doctor who, after giving me a morphine shot, scared me to death the next day by sending two officers out to our place with a vial of morphine and a syringe. Just the sight of the uniforms practically paralyzed me with the cop horrors, for I had no idea what the doctor had told them about me. Actually, he had simply asked them to deliver the narcotics as a precautionary measure. Although both were sympathetic and friendly, they left me so shaken with fear of arrest as a junkie that I didn't get over it for hours.

We had planned to stay in St. Petersburg for two weeks, but the weather and my constant pain drove us back north in six days. The first thing we did when we arrived home was to get rid of our wonderful old estate in Lamoine and move to Bar Harbor, where we rented a small house. Much as I hated to do it, I had no choice. Besides being too close to Ellsworth and too far from Bar Harbor, the Lamoine place was too expensive. With my income cut by more than half, I couldn't afford the payments.

Two weeks after we were settled in Bar Harbor, I was back on drugs again. As usual, I ignored my addiction and considered this only a pain-killing method. And, as usual, it was only a few days before the addiction overshadowed everything else. I was on morphine right from the start, shooting more and more each day and getting less and less relief. I could fake my way through the days, but the nights were hell. (In the early stages of any addictive period, a drug victim can appear normal to the uninitiated as long as his hunger for narcotics is satisfied.) I couldn't sit still without shots, and Seconal and other relaxants only aggravated the problem.

I endured it for about ten days before phoning Dr. Barr, who told me to see him as soon as I could. He wanted more comprehensive X rays. I would meet him in his office on Marlborough Street the next day, and we could have the X rays done at the Massachusetts General Hospital. Armed with plenty of morphine, which I had obtained by my various usual means, I had Kay drive me to the airport early so that I could shoot just before boarding the plane. For the same reason, I sent her right home without waiting to see me off.

The moment she left, I started for the men's room, but stopped when a man in a pearl-gray fedora and a heavy overcoat gave me the cop horrors. As I watched him reading a paper in the waiting area, I was certain that his only reason for being there was to catch me in the act of shooting. However, when he paid no attention to me, I edged my way into the men's room, got into a pay toilet, gave myself a shot, and went back to the waiting area. I felt better when I saw that the man hadn't moved. He was sitting in the same place, still reading his paper.

I had another attack of the cop horrors when he boarded the same plane that I did. I watched him all the way to Portland, then sighed with relief when he deplaned there. Before we arrived in Boston, I had taken another shot, and I needed still a third the moment I checked into my room at the Statler-Hilton Hotel. By then, I had had half a dozen more attacks of the cop horrors, for I seemed to see federal narcotics agents everywhere I looked: on the airplane, in the Boston airport, in the taxi line. (I took a limousine to the hotel because I thought that surely a man nearby trying to hail a cab had been watching me.) The limousine passenger beside me, a well-dressed man in his fifties, tried to strike up a conversation with me, but my mumbling replies discouraged him, and we rode through the Sumner Tunnel and the city in silence. Not until he got off at the Parker House was I certain that he had no interest in me.

As I got out in front of my own hotel, followed the

doorman into the lobby, went to the desk to check in, and followed the bellhop to my room, there seemed to be federal people everywhere: a baby-faced young man waiting for someone in the lobby, an older man in a slouch hat at the information desk, a tall, distinguished-looking man waiting when we reached the elevator. I was shaking when that last one got on with us, but he stepped out of the elevator at a lower floor.

I shuffled like a thief in the night after the bellhop as he led me to my room, and quickly tipped him to get him out of there so I could take a shot. There was barely enough morphine left to fill the syringe, so I diluted it with hot water to save something for the next shot, which I knew I would need soon. I held back as long as I could on that one, my mind alive with junkie fears. I froze every time I heard footsteps in the corridor, relaxing only when they passed my door or when I heard another door slammed shut. I took the phone off the hook and put the "Do not disturb" sign on my door before taking the last shot. I looked at my watch. It was only 6:30 P.M. I wasn't due in Joe Barr's office until 10:00 the next morning.

Fifteen and a half hours, I thought. *How the hell can I make it without a fix? What can I do? Where can I go? I've got to look half decent or Joe will know I'm back on junk. I won't sleep. I'll be starting withdrawal by the time I see him. How can I handle this?*

I undressed, and, to my horror, noticed bloodstains on my T-shirt. My shoulders were dotted with tiny scars, souvenirs of addiction, for in order to get the junk circulating quickly you have to go deep. I had been shooting into the shoulders instead of the arms, legs, or hips, because those other veins were already showing the wear and tear of frequent shots, legitimate and otherwise. This is another common junkie problem: after a while, there is no easy place to shoot, and you have to hunt all over your body for areas that will take a needle. In a mental institution a few years later I had a junkie fellow patient with a wry sense of humor. We both had long since reached the point where we had more scars than places to shoot on our bodies, when an elderly man shuffled by, his arms blue with swollen veins.

"God, what a picnic a junkie could have on a pair of arms like that!" said my friend. "You couldn't live long enough to use up all those veins if you shot every hour twenty-four hours a day for ten years."

I hung the T-shirt on the back of a chair, making sure that the stains were showing so I would remember to get a new shirt in the morning before seeing Dr. Barr. I turned on the television, propped the pillows up, and sat on the bed, but I just couldn't concentrate—the bottom had fallen out of my life. All I could think about was the fix I didn't have. I stood up, paced, sat, lay down, then suddenly went into a momentary depression so intense that tears were running down my face. It's a feeling every junkie has when he's run out of anything to shoot. He combines the cop horrors with the horror of early withdrawal, although that doesn't really hit for twenty-four to forty-eight hours. Perhaps it isn't physiological at all, but just a feeling of utter desolation for want of a fix, because it lasts only a short time. Mine went on for perhaps fifteen minutes, although it seemed hours. It was just a little past 7:00 when the depression ended and the tears stopped flowing. Later, a junkie friend of mine who had been off drugs for seventeen years told me he had these little fits of depression every so often for six years after he kicked the habit. I had them myself for five months after I took the last shot of my life. They're some sort of reflex action that only junkies have. I have never known anyone addicted to anything else to have this reaction, once he had stopped taking whatever he had been on.

The longer I stayed in the room, the smaller it seemed. There are only so many places to go and things to do when you're alone in a hotel room, and I had covered them all a dozen times before I began to go stir-crazy. Out of junk, in the preliminary throes of unwanted withdrawal, fearful of discovery, mad with anxiety, my back and legs throbbing incessantly, I got into a hot tub. When that didn't help, I decided to try to drown my troubles. I took the bloodstained T-shirt off the chair and put it on along with the rest of my clothes, and, after poking my head out of the door to make sure the corridor was clear, went across the street to a liquor store, and bought a fifth of scotch.

I had never been much of a drinker, usually settling for a beer or two except on rare occasions when I became pleasantly plastered while entertaining or visiting friends. Years later, Karen told me of a childhood memory of coming over to kiss me goodnight before going to bed and remarking, "Daddy, you're drunk," but it was one of those situations an adult forgets and a child remembers. To this day I don't remember the incident, and was surprised to learn how deep an impression it had made upon my third-grader daughter.

Back in the Statler-Hilton, I took the bottle to my room, turned on the television set, undressed—putting the T-shirt back on the chair where I would see it in the morning—and poured myself a drink, half scotch, half water. I drained the glass so quickly that before leaving the bathroom I made another drink and carried it to bed, where I tried to relax while watching TV. Neither the liquor nor the program (a basketball game, I think) helped rid me of either pain or anxiety. I finished the bottle in less than an hour, but I might as well have been drinking straight water for all the effect it had upon me. After rejecting the idea of getting another fifth before the liquor store closed, I filled my syringe with hot water and gave myself a shot, in the hope that there were a few drops of morphine left. If so, they did no more good than the scotch. I finally took a couple of Seconal tablets, put out the lights, turned off the television, and tried to sleep.

Somewhere along the line, I might have dozed off for a few minutes, but all I can remember is suffering through one of the most terrifying nights of my life. The pain, the pacing, the almost uncontrollable desire for a fix, consumed me as the dull, dead hours passed: each minute a lifetime, each hour an eternity. Despite my discomfort, I never thought of going out to find a pusher, if, indeed, I had even known where to go. Although I had been in and out of Boston for years, I didn't know the city very well. Most of my time there had been spent either at the hospital or in a doctor's office.

As badly off as I was, I doubt if I would have sought a fix outside even if I had known where to find one. The whole idea of buying narcotics on the street appalled me. I suppose my biggest objection was a moral one: As a church-going Christian, I had been taught to distinguish right from wrong, and so because of their illegality I could never smoke pot or try LSD or any other hallucinatory drugs. Senseless as it may sound in view of my past history as a con artist and a narcotics thief who replaced pain-killing drugs with water to satisfy his addiction, this was a fork in the road to hell that I would not take. Pushers sold mostly heroin, which, like the others, is illegal. (So was stealing, but that didn't count, I rationalized, as long as what I stole wasn't.) Demerol, and most of the amphetamines and barbiturates, could be legally obtained and legally administered, which made them okay for me. This was illogical thinking, of course, but I was an active junkie, and no active junkie thinks any other way.

In the first light of dawn, I sighed with the relief of the damned about to be released from purgatory. *Only a few more hours,* I thought. *Joe will come up with something. He's the only person I know who appreciates the agony of spinal problems without ever having had them himself. He knows I can take a beating, but nobody can take one this bad. If there's a nonsurgical answer somewhere, he'll know that too. And if there isn't, he'll figure one out.*

It didn't make sense, of course. There was *no* answer. As great a humanitarian and surgeon as this man was, he couldn't perform miracles. But, as I was unable to think straight, it was natural for me to have almost as much faith in him as in the God to whom I prayed daily.

Painfully—for, because of my height, I had to lean down to see my face in the mirror—I shaved, but even after finishing I looked terrible. My cheeks were drawn, my eyes bloodshot, my nerves jumpy, my walk the shambling step of a semi-cripple. Leaving the bloody T-shirt on the chair, I dressed as quickly as I could and walked the streets within sight of the hotel until the shops opened. I stopped into a cafeteria for coffee, but couldn't get down more than a few sips. Just after 9:00 I went into a men's store for a new T-shirt, and returned to my room. After putting it on, I tore the old one to shreds and flushed it down the toilet, piece by piece.

Then I took a cab to Dr. Joe Barr's office.

VI

When a junkie has enough drugs to satisfy his needs, he usually is able to deal with straight people in a normal manner. Only a heavy user who has been at it a long time loses his ability to relate naturally to others. In the very early stages of withdrawal, forced or voluntary, addicts can roughly be divided into two categories—those who, no matter how miserable, can put on an act when the occasion demands, and those who can't.

Motivated partly by pride, partly by fear, and partly by desire for respect, I could put on a pretty good act in those first years of my addiction. My respect for Joe Barr was exceeded only by my desire for his respect for me. Much as it hurt physically and psychologically, I straightened up as I approached his office and gave myself a mental pep talk to act as though my only problem were pain, for I didn't want him to see signs of my much worse problem of addiction. Nor did I really wish to undergo extensive X rays; I was sure that I could handle Joe, but to withstand a strenuous day at the hospital in my condition would be beyond my capabilities. Besides, from a medical standpoint, I didn't think X rays would show anything new. Joe had suggested an X ray series for me, but I was certain that a man with his great sympathy for people in pain would not make me do anything

I didn't want to do, especially if it didn't seem absolutely essential.

Joe Barr was one of those rare medical geniuses who thought in human rather than technical terms. He was a great orthopedic surgeon, one of the foremost in the world, and people came from all over the world to seek his advice, treatment and, if necessary, surgical touch. To Joe, a patient was a person, and he treated each patient as such, somewhat in the manner of an old-fashioned general practitioner. Only his skill in the operating room was technical. In voice, manner, and courtesy, he was a human being, not a medical prima donna (as many outstanding surgeons are sometimes likely to be). A talk with him was worth a thousand pills or shots, for he gave you the feeling that the only thing on his mind was your discomfort and his only desire, to alleviate it.

When I entered his office, although he must have noticed my haggard, obviously abnormal appearance, Joe gave no sign of being aware that I had been back on drugs. He accepted my explanation that it was due only to pain, and agreed that there was nothing to be gained by my going through a series of X rays. He did have a few X rays of my lumbar region taken in his office, and studied them in my presence after they were developed. But most of the time he just talked— about me, the family, the situation at Bar Harbor, and his own hope that I might be more comfortable by setting up a program alternating two weeks of work with two weeks of bed rest. In the hour that I spent with him, we didn't mention drugs, he prescribed none and I asked for none. As we talked—he in his gentle voice, I in my booming bass—I made a mental note never to let narcotics get the better of me again. I would go though this withdrawal cold turkey, and once off I would stay off.

One of the last things Joe said was, "Jim, if you find you

can't stand this any longer, don't let it get out of hand. There is a last resort which might be helpful."

"What's that?" I asked.

"Our paraplegic ward in the White Building of the Massachusetts General Hospital."

"Paraplegic ward?"

"Don't let the word scare you. You're not a paraplegic and never will be. But I think you can benefit from the same type of therapy our people give to paraplegics."

"What makes you think so?" I didn't mean that to sound like a challenge, but I guess it did. The whole idea of going into a paraplegic ward repelled me.

"Your legs are affected, Jim," he said. "We don't know yet how much. I think what happens in the next few months may tell us. You won't stand still during that period—you'll either go up or down. If you go up, fine. But if you don't use your legs much because of the pain, you'll run the danger of atrophy, and the longer you wait, the harder the rehabilitation will be. You don't have to be a paraplegic for paraplegic therapy to help you, and the best place for that is in the White Building."

Annoyed at the prospect, I said, "Joe, why do you keep saying 'will' instead of 'would'? It sounds as if you expect me to get worse."

"I don't know what to expect," he said, gently. "I just want you to be aware of the possibility of atrophy in your legs, and to know there's a good chance that it can be eliminated."

He went on for several minutes, his voice, his manner, his obviously deep concern so genuine that I was ashamed of my own show of impatience. When I apologized, Joe lifted one hand as if to wave away the whole incident.

"Forget it, Jim," he said. "You don't have to apologize for

not wanting to go into a paraplegic ward even if it seems necessary. I agree, the prospect is frightening, but it really isn't that bad. In fact—and again I say this applies only to *if*, not *when* you might go—the experience will help you because you'll see people all around you in much worse shape than you are. *If* you go," again he stressed the "if" in order to reassure me. "I think you'll help others as well as yourself. You're a doctor with compassion, empathy, and a sincere interest in the well-being of your fellow man."

Later, when we parted, I realized that Joe had made me so well aware of the possibilities that might result from my disability that I was ready to face anything—in fact, he had me almost *wanting* to go into the paraplegic ward. As always, he had said the right things in the right way. A wise man, Dr. Joe Barr. He's gone now, but his heritage is the indelible imprint of his sympathy, kindness, and knowledge of human nature and human suffering upon the thousands of patients whose privilege it was to come under his care. He made life a little more bearable for every sufferer, including the permanently handicapped, who came in contact with him.

But, once away from him, I allowed my own problems to rise to the surface again. Although I knew I was in for a rough two weeks of withdrawal, I went through it so well that I thought I had kicked drugs for good, but I was wrong, for I was on a rapidly downhill physical course, spending more time off my feet than on them. The pain of dragging myself around was more than I could stand, and almost as soon as withdrawal ended, I began shooting again. It did little good, because my difficulty in walking couldn't be alleviated by drugs. I managed to get through the summer by spending most of my time in bed or as a patient in the Mt. Desert Island Hospital, where others could help a little, by controlling my drug intake, for instance. But I lost ground so steadily that when the doctor taking care of me in Bar Harbor suggested calling Joe Barr again, I told him to go ahead, even though I knew what it would mean.

In late September, 1958, I went by ambulance from Bar Harbor to Boston. Kay, who rode with me although she was seven months pregnant with Julie, gave me a shot of Demerol every two hours. We talked quite a bit, mostly about my illness, and she showed no animosity. It was one of the last times I can remember anything resembling real understanding between us.

The trip, which took nearly ten hours, was otherwise a nightmare. By the time we arrived at the hospital, I had sunk into a deep depression that hung on for days after I was admitted via the emergency room. While Kay checked me in, I was put through the regular routine, then taken up to the paraplegic-quadraplegic ward. Dr. Tom DeLorme, who had helped take care of me preoperatively and postoperatively when Joe Barr performed my last fusion, was in charge of me, since Tom specialized in orthopedic surgery and sub-specialized in muscle rehabilitation. (He later suffered disc problems that required much the same series of operations that I had undergone.)

Upon arrival in the ward I was nearly nauseated by the sight of about fifteen other patients, para- and quadraplegics, almost all of whom, as Joe had pointed out, were worse off than I. But when I first went in there, they had the opposite effect from what Joe had suggested. Instead of encouraging me, the scene deepened my depression. The thought of undergoing therapy in such a gloomy atmosphere made me feel sorrier than ever for myself.

My therapy began after a day of neurological tests to determine what I could and couldn't do. While I lay flat on my back, each leg was lifted by the therapist, a very strong, good-humored young woman about six feet tall. She raised each of my legs to find out how much restriction there was, due to either pain or atrophy. I could lift each leg myself about four inches, and only slightly more with her help. I could also walk a few steps—just about enough to go to the bathroom, so I didn't need a bedpan. Except for that and my daily therapy sessions, I wasn't out of bed at all for about three weeks. There was nothing wrong with me from the waist up; I could use my hands and arms normally—could feed myself, write, and hold a book or magazine in order to read. I slept fairly well after a rough first week, during which I was too depressed to sleep more than an hour or two at night. Once I became used to the place and friendly with some of the other patients, my depression receded and I slept better.

The human body has many muscles that normally don't function, but can do at least part of the job when something cripples or kills active muscles; it takes a therapist to start these dormant muscles functioning. However, even a top-notch therapist can do only so much. The patient himself has to do the rest—a long, slow, maddening process requiring confidence, determination, and complete cooperation with the therapist.

My therapy began with passive stretching of the muscles, stretching them to tolerance by putting each leg on the tall woman's shoulder and letting her gently but firmly move it more and more each day. It caused hard pain, so intense that in the first couple of weeks I had Demerol every three or four hours. Although the drugs helped a bit, they didn't eliminate the pain, but simply enabled me to handle it. Under such supervision as I had, they worked quite well, partly because of my own high threshold of pain and partly because I was grateful for any relief, no matter how slight.

The exercise room, right next to the ward, had machines for strengthening muscles and building up affected parts of the body, so that a patient could develop maximum use of whatever muscles he had left that could be developed. A few weeks after I entered the hospital, I began working in the exercise room under the therapist's direction. By this time we had become good friends, often kidding each other about our respective heights, since we were both unusually tall, I for a man, she for a woman. Her size didn't detract from her general appearance; she was as attractive as she was sympathetic. I'm sure her height caused her no paucity of dates or any of the mental grief that comes with it for a woman of her age, which was somewhere in the twenties.

"The world is full of guys over six feet tall," she said one day. "It takes just a few to have a good time and only one to marry."

"You'll have six-foot children," I quipped.

"What's so bad about that?" she retorted. "My parents did."

This sort of banter makes for a good therapist, and she was. Humor is an essential part of therapy. Even a quadraplegic with no hope of recovery will accept his handicap a little better if the therapist can make him laugh. An occasional look at the lighter side of life is all he needs to keep from going mad.

My therapist tested my muscle strength on a machine that measured total leg pull, which in my case increased a bit every day after I got over the initial shock of being part of a group of desperately handicapped people. Although the upper part of my body was nearly normal, she continually tested that, too, putting a harness on my shoulders to measure my flexion strength and extension strength. This was the first time I had ever seen this therapy in use, and it deeply interested me both as a doctor and a human being. The woman spent half an hour twice a day with me, telling me what she wanted me to do and, knowing that I was a doctor, explaining to me the mechanics and purposes of everything that had to be done.

While the work was serious, the kidding went on all the time that I was in the ward—just about three months. Once, when some of the stretching exercises were particularly painful, I joked, "Why the hell didn't you go into wrestling where you could make a lot more money than you do now by torturing poor guys like me?"

"Because wrestlers take themselves too seriously," she said. "Especially female wrestlers. And some are bigger than I am, and could probably beat me too easily. You're a big, strong man, but I always know I can beat you. It's good for my ego."

She knew just how far she could go, and never overstepped the bounds of good taste and good humor. She worked under Tom DeLorme, who came to see me every day, and sometimes watched the therapy, occasionally making suggestions that he thought might be helpful. She followed his instructions to the letter, always doing exactly what he told her to do.

Those three months in the paraplegic ward of the Massachusetts General Hospital taught me more about human nature than I would have learned in three years anywhere else. No matter how badly handicapped, every person there had something for which to be thankful—close family ties, a little daily progress, new interests, new hopes, plans for new skills within his own physical limits. It wasn't long before I realized just how tough the human spirit is, just what hope—real hope—means. I entered that ward desperately sorry for myself; because of the people I met, some of whom became my close friends, I left there counting my blessings. Even today, nearly fifteen years later, I can draw inspiration from some of my associations there.

There was a little redheaded boy of almost twelve, paralyzed from the waist down when an older brother accidentally shot him with a .22 rifle. The bullet split in half after hitting him in the shoulder. One half collapsed one of his lungs, the other half severed the spinal cord. A cheerful youngster with wavy hair and a constant grin on his freckled face, he zoomed around the ward in his wheelchair, beeping a bicycle horn that one of the other patients had given him. He cheered up the whole ward with his good humor, he never made a nuisance of himself, and he was so considerate and perceptive that he seemed to know instinctively when to talk to certain people and when to leave them alone.

His own condition seemed to be the last thing on his mind, although the little guy was in pretty bad shape. About every two weeks he had to be packed in ice to keep his fever down below a temperature that would have destroyed his brain, and to keep kidney stones from forming in his urinary tract. Because of his soaring fever and his repeated development of kidney stones, he had no control of any of his bodily functions. To this day I don't know what happened to him, although I'm afraid he didn't live very long.

Then there was the hemiplegic (paralyzed on one side) bartender, a cheerful, friendly man who was always giving people a mental lift with his fund of funny little stories about the more colorful of his customers. Besides our love of singing, we had something in common that was unusual in the ward: he and I were the only people there not permanently handicapped. He had had what appeared to be a stroke from a brain abscess caused by a staph infection, which started with a boil on his arm. He hadn't paid much attention to it, but one day he fell while getting out of the bathtub, and couldn't get up. He didn't know just what had happened, but when he couldn't move his arm and leg on one side, he assumed that he had a stroke. Evidently, from what his doctor told me, the arm infection had drained into his bloodstream, developing into blood-poisoning, which probably first hit his chest, then his head. In his head there was a sudden rupture resulting in generalized pressure, which caused his hemiplegia. A spinal tap showed pus in the path to the brain and, since the doctors couldn't treat him with antibiotics, they had to open his skull and drain off the staph infection. Eventually, he recovered completely, and, in fact, left the hospital about a week before I did.

And there was my closest friend of all in the ward, Bob Hawks, a wonderful guy from Maine. Quite a devout fellow, he was church soloist in the biggest church in Portland. He considered his accident simply an unfortunate act of God that would not stop him from accomplishing his purpose. Although he was grievously paralyzed, he never lost confidence in himself, and served as an inspiration to us all. Once an outstanding athlete, he had also been a good teacher of almost all sports. He had trained his six-year-old daughter to ski so well that she was already going on advanced slopes with him.

Bob had been an athletic director in Portland, but, unable to receive fulfillment from that occupation, he had started a home for kids from broken homes, a place he called Opportunity Farm. He loved this humanitarian work, because through it he succeeded in finding his niche.

On the night before he was hurt, he told me, he and his wife were discussing their way of life and the satisfaction he derived from seeing homeless boys moving in the right direction and keeping out of trouble. He had about thirty-five kids in his school, the money to run it was coming in steadily from charitable organizations and interested individuals, and he looked forward to a long, productive career of helping kids of all ages develop into useful, productive citizens. The last thing he said to his wife that night was, "Nobody deserves to be as happy as I am. I often wonder why life has been so good to me." The next day he was putting baled hay on an overhead lift that automatically hoisted the bales into a hay mow, when he noticed the lift slipping. It was about to crash down on a boy standing under it. He dove for the youngster and shoved him out of the way just as the lift let go. Before he could move, the lift hit him between the shoulder blades, driving a vertebra into his spinal cord, severing the cord so that he was paralyzed through the lower chest level on down. He could use his arms, but not his lower chest muscles or legs, and he had no bladder or bowel control.

He had been in therapy a long time when I arrived in the ward, but there wasn't much that could be done to help him. The loss of his chest muscles prevented him from learning to walk with crutches. God knows, he tried hard enough. Many people with two useless legs can propel themselves along by swinging forward with the power coming from their arms and the girdle muscles around the waist. Braces lock their legs, which are strapped together stretched out, and their arm, girdle, and chest muscles give them the strength for swing-through walking. But without those girdle and chest muscles, Bob couldn't generate enough strength in the upper part of his body to swing his weight. He must have been terribly frustrated, because he tried so hard and failed so often, but he never gave the slightest indication of impatience or discouragement.

He went home to Maine two weeks before I did. The night before he left, I was lying on my own bed thinking about him and wondering how he'd be able to handle the kids at his school, if at all, when he yelled from his bed about twelve feet from me, "Hey, Jim, how about coming over and shooting the breeze with me for a little while?"

The attendant had just put him into bed from his wheelchair. As usual, he was hooked up to a catheter irrigation system, which not only served as an outlet for bodily waste matter, but kept bladder stones from forming. When I got out of bed and walked over to him, I thought of his wife who had often come to the hospital to learn her part in his rehabilitation. It seemed she had nothing much to look forward to but a life of hard work and constant frustration. Yet I knew she could handle it, for she was a strong-minded, cheerful woman with the same type of quiet confidence that Bob had. Some people would have dreaded the responsibility, if, indeed, they could have accepted it at all, but this couple were two of a kind, and their deep love for each other was obvious and touching.

When I reached Bob's bed, he said, "Do you mind pulling the curtains around the bed?" After I had, he said, "You know, Jim, something's been bugging me about going home."

"What is it?" I said, although I thought I knew. Here was a guy about 32 years old who loved sports and all the pleasures of the outdoor life. He had been an athlete, had trained half a dozen beagle hounds to go with him when he hunted, loved to fish, had played baseball, football, and basketball, and had boxed. Now he was going home to a life that, because of his lack of bladder and bowel control, would mean going to bed in the middle of the day so his wife could hook up his catheter and irrigation system—and he wouldn't even be able to get into bed himself. He couldn't walk, had no sexual function, and would have to be helped in and out of the wheelchair in which he would live from now on.

Yes, I thought I knew what was bugging him.

"The thing that really bothers me most," he said, "is that people will think I'm faking. My wife will drive into town and have to help me out of the car and into a wheelchair, and people will say, 'Look at that lazy bum. If he had any courage he'd be walking on crutches just like any other paraplegic.' I can see them now, watching me take advantage of my wife, making her do all the work while I'm sitting in the wheelchair or lying in bed doing nothing."

"That's right," I said. "Some people—not all, but some—will look at you and say and think exactly those things. But you know differently, I know differently, your wife knows differently, and so do all the other people who know what you've been through. I faced it myself. People would give that disgusted look, and I could almost hear them saying, 'Look at that big, strapping hulk of a man who claims he's in pain all the time. It's just an excuse to stay in bed whenever he feels like it. Nobody that size could be that uncomfortable.' I stood up to it pretty well, and you'll stand up to it better because you have more inner strength than I have."

We talked for a couple of hours, I guess, before I went back to my own bed. I knew a few things about Bob he didn't know himself, one of which was that his legs would probably have to be amputated sooner or later because some calcium had already formed in them, and more would form as time went on. Eventually, the circulation would be cut off and gangrene would set in. Yet he was so cheerful, so confident, so sure he could cope, that I truly envied him. A man with such spirit, such dedication, such love of life, could cope with anything.

Many years later, I ran into a minister from Bangor at a drug seminar I was conducting on Cape Cod. When he told me he had gone to Bangor from Portland, I asked about Bob

Hawks. His face lit up as he said, "One of the most wonderful men I have ever known."

"Is he still alive?" I asked.

"Alive? He's not only alive, but teaching speech therapy to handicapped kids. He drives his own station wagon, gets in and out of it himself, and takes care of all his personal needs. He's an outstanding swimmer who has won para-Olympic championships every year for the past ten."

"Does he still have his legs?"

"Oh, yes," the minister said. "What an inspiration that man is! Maybe it sounds trite quoting a classic line from English poetry, but *there* is somebody about whom it can be truthfully said, 'To know him is to love him.' And I consider knowing him one of the great privileges of my life."

"Does he . . . wonder if people think he's faking?"

"Maybe he did once, but he doesn't anymore. There's no reason for it now. Everyone who knows him knows what he has accomplished, not just for himself but for other people."

"I wish I could be like him," I said.

The minister looked at me, then said, slowly, "In a way, Dr. DeWitt, you are."

I consider that to be the finest tribute anyone has ever paid me.

VII

I thought my troubles were over when I returned home after my discharge from the Massachusetts General Hospital paraplegic ward in late December, 1958. The therapist had done such a good job that I could walk normally and was nearly free from pain. However, about two days before I left, I started to feel pain in my right armpit, where there was a small, hard, inflamed lump. The hospital's specialist in internal medicine, whom I knew well, recognized it as a staph infection of a type that had been running through most of the Boston hospitals. Since antibiotics couldn't control it, he had me put hot salt solutions on it and told me to be sure to let him know if it didn't improve. It didn't, but I was so eager to get home for Christmas that I wouldn't mention it. If I did they wouldn't have let me out on schedule. Of all the stupid decisions I have ever made in my life, this was one of the worst. By going home prematurely, I not only risked blood-poisoning, but exposed everyone in the family to the same thing, since my condition was extremely contagious. I flew to Bar Harbor on December 23, five days after Julie, our fourth and last child, was born. My father met me at the airport, and, despite the staph infection, I picked up Kay and Julie, who were still in the hospital, the next day.

I woke up Christmas morning in such agony that I called

the Mt. Desert Island Hospital, and they told me to come in that night. On any other day but Christmas, I would have gone right in, because that node under my arm had grown to the size of a baseball. However, I delayed a couple of days, and once in the hospital, I stayed two and a half months, undergoing five operations before the staph cleared up. How nobody in my family picked the infection up, I'll never know. They were all exposed to it.

Since I had to remain in bed throughout my hospital stay and wasn't allowed to do my therapeutic exercises because any movement might have triggered blood-poisoning, I couldn't walk at all by the time the staph was cured. In the meantime, the doctors treating me, who knew of my addiction, were very cautious in giving me drugs, keeping me down to one-sixth grain of morphine a couple of times a day when the pain was severe, and alternating medication as much as possible. At one point, I was getting morphine, Demerol, Dilaudid, and Pantopon in small but steady doses. The doctors then tapered me off all narcotics in the usual manner, and I was drug-free by the time they sent me home. At last, I seemed to be on an upward path.

That didn't last long. With an open wound under my arm—although the staph was cured—I had to keep applying antiseptic salve and staying clear of the children for another month and a half until the wound closed. In the meantime, I resumed the therapy I had learned at the Massachusetts General Hospital. While it helped me regain strength in the legs it was very painful, and I still couldn't resume my medical practice. To add to my problems, I was up to my ears in debt—owing something like $40,000 in medical bills. I did get a break in selling some property to the state, which needed the land for a new road going through there; for that I collected $25,000, all of which went toward my bills, but I still owed about fifteen thousand dollars and had no idea where to get the money. That was exclusive of my huge debt to my father, who sometimes borrowed money to help me out. Naturally, he never asked me for it, but I knew he could use whatever I might pay, and I felt a deeper moral obligation to him than to anyone else.

Needing an escape from reality once again, I turned to the only escape I knew. I started with a normal dose of 100 mgs. of Demerol or a quarter grain of morphine, sometimes by mouth, sometimes by hypo. As usual, this snowballed very rapidly over a period of three weeks. I thought that Kay didn't suspect anything, until one morning when she woke me up and told me that she had just finished cleaning up blood in the bathroom and that I had a cut on my scalp. I had taken 200 mgs. of Demerol and a couple of sleeping pills the night before, and then blacked out. I must have gotten up to go to the bathroom and then slipped while I was there, but that's only a guess because I had no memory of it. Kay and I had words when I denied taking anything except one sleeping pill. I didn't come close to convincing her. She was really angry, and I was completely on the defensive. From then on, I knew I would never again be able to take drugs without her knowledge. Aside from that, I was frightened because of my blackout. That had never happened to me before, and was, in fact, another step on my road to hell; I knew it wouldn't be long before I would be having blackouts regularly, and I had no idea what Kay might do then.

I tried to withdraw, but couldn't, and there I was, back on the same old merry-go-round. Three nights later I knocked myself out with another combination of narcotics and sleeping pills, and was so far gone that my wife couldn't wake me up. I have no idea what time it was, and I'm not sure why she tried to get me up in the middle of the night, because she never told me. My guess is that my breathing was too shallow for her to hear and all she could feel was a faint heartbeat. Whatever the reason, she called Dr. George Wood, who was within easy reach, since we had returned to Brewer when I left Mt. Desert Island Hospital after getting over my staph infection. I woke up in a straitjacket, with my wrists and ankles strapped to the bed, in what looked to me like a violent ward, since the patients, mostly in straitjackets, were screaming, sobbing, and yelling all around me. I soon learned that I was in the medical psychotic ward of the Veterans Hospital in Togus, Maine.

After a while, a heavy-set, grim-looking female doctor came over to my bed and, without any preliminaries, snapped, "How much narcotics have you been taking?"

"What am I doing here?" I said. "And why am I strapped down?"

"I'll ask the questions."

"Okay," I said, "I'll answer them. But first untie me."

She studied a card in her hand, then said, "Are you really a doctor?"

"Yes. And I'm a damn sick doctor. I've been in pain for years. I couldn't hurt anyone if I wanted to, so how about getting me out of this thing?"

Without a word, she released my wrists and legs, took off the straitjacket, and, while I flexed my arm and leg muscles, said, "Let's start all over. How much narcotics have you been taking?"

"None."

"Don't try to kid me. You're committed here as a drug addict."

"Who committed me?"

"Your wife."

Surprised and resentful, I said, "She committed me as an addict?"

"You bet she did. Now, tell me what you've been taking and how much."

"I have terrible back pain. I might have taken a little Demerol."

"By mouth or hypo?"

Knowing now that I couldn't con her, I told her the truth—or, at least, most of it.

"It helps me more when I shoot," I said. "I'm in pain now and need something."

"Well, you're not going to get anything."

"Doctor, I've got hard pain in my back and legs. I've had several operations, including a fusion of all five of my lumbar vertebrae."

I looked around the ward and shuddered. "Whose idea was it to put me in here?"

"We have no other facilities for alcoholics or drug addicts."

"I'm not an addict. Maybe I took a little too much last night, but I'm not an addict. How long do I have to stay here?"

"You'll get a hearing within six days," she said. "It won't matter what you say, because both your wife and your doctor reported that you were knocked out from drugs. After the hearing you'll be here for 30 days, then in an open ward for another 30, and finally in another ward for the last 30."

"That's 90 days altogether."

"Right."

"Well, I'm not staying here 90 days."

"How long you stay here won't be your decision."

I looked around the ward again. Patients were moaning and groaning, or just jabbering senselessly. A few, physically unrestrained, were rocking back and forth or bouncing up and down on their beds. There were strong odors of offal and urine. I later learned that very few had bladder or bowel control, and that every two hours during the night the lights were turned on so that patients could be scrubbed down and rinsed off with alcohol.

"Really, doctor," I said, "You can't honestly believe I belong in this place."

"Maybe you don't, but where else can we put you? A drug addict is a criminal."

"I'm *not* a drug addict," I interrupted.

"You *are*. You're lucky you're not in jail," she said, then turned and walked away.

The ward, which was locked, looked like a scene out of Dante's *Inferno*, an assortment of poor devils living in worlds of their own. Not since medical school had I ever seen a place like it. Each patient was "doing his own thing," and no two people seemed even to gravitate toward each other. Except for doctors and attendants coming and going, to feed or clean people up, they paid no attention to me, the only person with whom I could communicate was a young alcoholic from Boston, whose bed was about three feet away from mine. We both were suffering through withdrawal, he from booze and I from drugs, but we could converse rationally from time to time, although the first two days in the ward were hell for us both.

My own withdrawal was slightly easier than usual because I had been back on drugs only a few weeks before my commitment. However, I couldn't eat much. Everything, including water, seemed to taste salty, and my sense of smell was so acute that all odors seemed acrid to me. Drug addiction distorts the senses to the point of hypersensitivity. While you are on drugs, food tastes all right to you, but when you stop you have bare, stark sensory and motor effects. Even smoking (to which I am still a slave) gives you no pleasure and fails to relieve tension. Every cigarette I smoked tasted awful.

On my second day in the ward, the alcoholic asked me if I had been committed. After I said, "Yes," he said, "You're going to your hearing, aren't you?"

"No."

"Why not?"

"The doctor said it wouldn't do any good."

"Don't listen to her. You have the right to go by law, you're rational, and you'll make a good impression."

"How am I going to get there?"

"The hospital must provide transportation," he said. "That's also the law."

Later that day when the female doctor, accompanied by the head of the psychiatric department, came over to talk to me, I asked to go to the hearing. Both told me that it would be a waste of time. When I insisted, they said they didn't have any way of getting me to Bangor, where my hearing would take place before the city council. This was standard procedure in Maine—hearings of this type were conducted by the city council of the patient's home town. I cited the law and demanded transportation. After some fussing and arguing, the head doctor said he'd see what he could do. Then he added, "If they release you, it would be the worst thing that could happen to you."

"Why?"

"Because you'll never be cured if you don't stay here 90 days."

"Well," I said, "I certainly don't need 30 in *this* ward."

"That's the rule for all addicts."

"I'm not an addict. I just took too much to relieve my pain."

"Dr. DeWitt," he said, "you *are* an addict, and you know it. If you get out now, you'll just go back on drugs."

He tried again to talk me out of going to the hearing, but I stuck to my guns. I wasn't kidding anybody, including my-self, about not being an addict, but I really didn't believe that just staying in the hospital 90 days would do me any good. They didn't know how to treat addicts—nobody knew much about it at the time, and they know precious little now—and I knew that simply moving from ward to ward in an institution for three months would be useless. I firmly believed then, as I do today, that, without therapy of any kind, such a long hospital stay couldn't help at all.

By the day of the hearing, which was to be held early in the evening, I had arranged my transportation—a station wagon with two attendants and a driver. The head doctor told me to call and tell him the result of the hearing; he wanted to know either way. The trip to Bangor from Togus was pleasant. The attendants were good guys who, after talk-ing to me and realizing that I was quite rational, told me I shouldn't have any trouble breaking the commitment. My withdrawal was nearly over, and, except for some back and leg pains, I felt pretty good.

Kay was in the lobby with George Wood and another doc-tor friend of mine. She was cool, but not nasty. George and the other doctor, genuinely glad to see me looking and acting normal, asked me a few questions about my physical condi-tion and mental attitude, then asked about the hospital. I told them truthfully that the situation there was hopeless for me, and why I thought so. Like most doctors, they had no idea about the nature of life in a mental ward, since they never came in close contact with any patients who might be sent to one. While Kay stayed with me in the lobby, the two doctors went to talk to the City Council. They returned half an hour later, to tell me the commitment had been with-drawn on their recommendation, so that there was no further need for a hearing. The guys who had taken me to Bangor shook my hand, congratulated me, and left. When I phoned the doctor at Togus and told him I was no longer committed, he said, "I think you should come back voluntarily."

"No, thank you," I said. "I've seen all I want of that place."

On the advice of the two doctors, and with Kay's approval, I spent that night in a private hospital in Bangor, a small but well-run place where I had taken care of many alcoholics when I practiced there. The next day, also at the doctors' suggestion, I phoned a psychiatrist in Washington, D.C., one of my former professors, who had for some reason changed his name from Katzenellenbogen to Katzenelbogen. He was a nice old guy, he's dead now, and I really think he helped me a little, despite a bad start. He had told me over the phone that he was arranging for me to enter a new private hospital in Washington, where he would come to see me every day and try to determine whether or not I was really a drug addict.

Because Kay didn't want to leave the children for the three weeks I was due to be in Washington, I flew down with a paid attendant whom I needed to make sure that I didn't take an overdose of drugs. He gave me Seconal every hour, and I was in pretty good shape when I got off the plane. We took a cab from the airport to the hospital, where I checked in and was taken to a small locked ward. The minute I heard the door slam shut, I knew that this place wasn't for me. Fed up with locked wards, I immediately started to plan ways of getting out of there.

My only hope was to talk Dr. Katzenelbogen into letting me out. As a private patient admitted on a voluntary basis, I had no trouble convincing a nurse to let me use the phone. When I got Dr. Katzenelbogen on the line, he said that he thought I should stay in the hospital, but he had no objection to my leaving after I told him that the months I had already been in hospitals were about all that I could take. I said that I'd check into a motel near his office and call him when I got there, and asked if he would come by for breakfast the next morning. After wavering a little, he finally told me that I had better spend the night in the hospital and leave the next day after he had seen me. I agreed, but afterwards told the head nurse that Dr. Katzenelbogen had said he wanted to see me in two hours. After asking a few questions to make sure that I had actually spoken to him, she released me, and I went to a motel near the Naval Hospital in Bethesda. When I called the doctor from there, he was slightly annoyed, but told me that it was all right, and that he would be in to see me that night.

Deciding to relax with a couple of drinks, I went to a nearby liquor store and bought two bottles of beer and one of wine. I took them back to the room with me, and after a short while I knocked myself out, the first time I had ever blacked out from liquor. Several hours later, the doctor woke me with a phone call from the motel office, and my head was spinning when he finally walked into the room. A kind, conscientious man, he said that perhaps it would be better for him to see me the next morning when I had sobered up.

I drank heavily all the time that I was in Washington; that was the first real indication that I might have an alcoholic as well as a drug problem. I didn't know if there was any correlation between the two, but at the time I had never heard of an alcoholic drug addict and didn't think it was possible for anyone to be one. The problem nearly threw poor old Dr. Katzenelbogen. After four days of trying to give me therapy through my alcoholic haze, he finally phoned Kay, and she agreed to ask my mother to take care of the children so that she could come down to see me. Although the doctor begged me to try staying sober until she arrived, I was out cold and later remembered nothing about her arrival. Kay also knew Dr. Katzenelbogen—in fact, she had been treated by him years before—and asked him what could be done about my drinking. There wasn't much anyone could do, but I did manage to cut down to a few beers a day and to stop drinking as heavily as before.

As I look back on it now, I'm not sure that my alcoholism had really developed by then, because I could stop drinking whenever I wanted to. I used liquor mainly as a substitute for drugs, a purpose that it did serve, since I took no drugs at all in Washington. I think my trouble was pretty much as the doctor had diagnosed it after having spoken with me every morning for three weeks: I was still reacting badly to the Togus experience—my cold turkey withdrawal there, my fight to be released, the quick moves into three hospitals within three days, and my recurrent back and leg pains. All this had caused severe emotional trauma, which, for the moment at least, could be somewhat alleviated by moderate amounts of booze.

I told the doctor nearly everything, leaving out only the amount of drugs I had been taking. Actually, I was conning myself—looking for a miracle cure, as most people do when they go to a psychiatrist. I was hoping he would give me some incredible formula that would eradicate my desire for drugs, but of course that couldn't happen, not even if I had admitted to being addicted.

After two weeks, Dr. Katzenelbogen decided I was neither a drug addict nor an alcoholic, and we started planning my future. I would return to Brewer, take the therapy I had learned at the Massachusetts General Hospital, maintain just enough of a drug intake to keep the pain level down, and, after a few months, resume my practice as a general practitioner rather than an anesthesiologist. In that way, I could make a sufficient living to support my family and pay off my debts, including those to my father. It was a beautiful plan, but a pipe dream: The day I arrived home I shot some Demerol, and within a week was taking any drug I could get my hands on.

On a night that still remains a barely discernible haze in my memory, I took another overdose of drugs and sleeping pills, and this time woke up with aching shoulders from battling the restraints of a straitjacket on the floor of a ward in the Bangor State Mental Hospital. I thought at first that Kay had committed me again, but this time it had been George Wood. He later told me that he would have mentioned it to me first, but he thought it better that I get right into the hospital before I killed myself with an overdose. During the thirteen days I was there, I went through withdrawal without too much sweat because, as at Togus, I had been on drugs only a short time. On the day I left, the hospital superintendent offered me a job as a medical consultant, which I accepted. It worked out very well.

This was the first time I had ever worked with psychiatric patients. My medical consultations with them did not consume too much time, so I started to pick out additional patients whom I thought I might be able to help. Soon, most of the staff psychiatrists were asking me to see some of their patients, with whom they felt they couldn't spend enough time. Everything went smoothly for three months, during which I took no drugs and drank only an occasional beer. Soon after I began working, I was put in charge of ordering the hospital's drugs. I knew that this was a dangerous situation, but I appreciated the superintendent's confidence in me, and during those three months I never exploited it.

One day a drug salesman, whom I knew from the Eastern Maine General, came to see me. He was a good man who knew his business, and we talked at length about what he had to sell and what new synthetics I might find useful. He finally left with me a large assortment of samples—including some amphetamines and barbiturates—suggesting that I try them on patients and ask other staff doctors to do the same. The salesman, of course, had assumed that I would turn them in to the hospital pharmacy, but I had such a busy schedule that afternoon that I didn't have time to do so. Instead, I left them in a drawer of my desk, and, for the moment, thought no more about them.

I went to the hospital the next morning with ambivalent feelings. I knew I should turn the stuff in to the pharmacy or I might be tempted to take some. On the other hand, I was reluctant to give it up because it represented a form of security to me. I decided it would do no harm to keep it in my desk, and for several days I didn't even open the drawer. Some time later, after a long, tiring day, I took a couple of the amphetamines, with results that were not unpleasant. They served as a pick-me-up, and I viewed them as nothing more than that. Although I was playing with fire and knew it, I still couldn't make myself take those drugs out of my desk and to the pharmacy where they belonged.

It didn't take long for me to start snowballing again, taking a steady dosage of amphetamines to keep me going during the day, and barbiturates to help me sleep at night. This time I couldn't even blame it on the pain, because that wasn't severe enough. Eventually I began calling in sick, first missing a day here and a day there, later missing two or three days in a row, and finally not coming in for a week. By that time, the superintendent knew that I was back on drugs and asked me to resign, which I did. That set me off on another cycle, not only of amphetamines and barbiturates, but narcotics as well, and this time I suddenly took off on a mad trip in search of something that I should have known couldn't be found simply by changes of scenery. I told Kay that I was seeking psychiatric help elsewhere, and left.

First I flew to Cuyahoga Falls, with the vague idea of getting a job in Akron or Cleveland, but ended up spending two days in my parents' house and then flying back to Brewer. I then decided to see Dr. Katzenelbogen and headed for Washington, but never got there. For some reason, I left the plane in Boston, checked into a downtown hotel, and, without calling any of my doctor friends there, decided to withdraw from drugs by using liquor as a substitute. I don't remember how much I drank. All I know is that once I began, I couldn't stop—the second warning sign that my addiction wasn't confined to drugs. In the two or three days I spent in Boston I must have packed away at least two bottles of booze every 24 hours.

Somewhere along the line, I managed to stop long enough to understand that if I didn't get home I'd wind up on Skid Row. I called Kay, and she in turn phoned my old neighbor and close friend, Reed Davis, who subsequently drove her down to get me. She was ice-cold to me when they arrived. On the way back to Brewer, Reed tried to bridge the communication gap between us with some stories and jokes, but they didn't work at all. Kay was as aloof when we arrived home as when we had left Boston.

Kay went on ahead, while Reed helped me into the house. For the first of hundreds of times I reeked of booze, and needed a drink in the worst way. Instead of *killing* my desire for drugs I found—that time, at least—that alcohol *whetted* it. So now, instead of ending up with one addiction substituted for another, I found myself the victim of two addictions at once. They have stayed with me to this day.

VIII

IF nothing else, the Boston experience and the trip back to Brewer sobered me up to the extent that I could practice medicine for a short time in Bangor. It was then that I decided I would never again be able to function normally without intensive psychiatric help. Remorse and shame, the usual aftermath of withdrawal, led me to resolutions that I knew I couldn't keep, ambitions that I knew were beyond reach, desires for affection and respect that I knew I had long since lost, and intentions of ensuring my family's security with drug-free, alcohol-free work that I knew I couldn't perform indefinitely.

Another short but intense bout with drugs—this time amphetamines—convinced me that I had to make a radical move. Knowing of no psychiatrist in Maine who could help me, and afraid to go back to Boston or Washington (both of which only brought memories of disaster), I flew to Ohio, where I spoke to Rev. Donal Powers, minister of the United Church of Christ, a close friend of the family in Cuyahoga Falls. He arranged for me to see a Cleveland psychiatrist who knew nothing about me except what Don told him—that I had a drug problem and desperately needed the kind of help he could offer.

I went to Cleveland and presented my case to the doctor as

a problem basically of pain, which, of course, it had been originally. While not admitting my addicition, I said that I took drugs because I couldn't tolerate the anxiety which the pain caused me. At the doctor's suggestion I moved the family to Cuyahoga Falls, largely because he wanted me to undergo long-term therapy, including hypnosis for pain. A month later, after Kay had closed everything out in Brewer and brought the children to Ohio, I seemed well on the road to recovery.

I avoided drugs and alcohol, and faithfully kept appointments with the doctor for as long as I remained under his care—about two years. At first I saw him three times a week, mostly for pain-killing hypnosis. We later cut down to twice a week, and finally to once a week. By that time I was practicing self-hypnosis, a skill I had learned with difficulty, since I was not by nature a good hypnotic subject. I eventually developed fairly good self-hypnosis, but when the pain was too severe I couldn't get myself into a deep enough trance, and needed help from the doctor. In order to increase the depth of the trance he gave me intravenous mixtures of sodium amytal and amphetamines, which put me into a state of relaxation complete enough to relieve the pain in my legs, yet were not strong enough to produce too deep a hypnotic sleep. Until near the end of the time I was under the doctor's care, I don't recall a single serious temptation to go back to drugs or alcohol.

In order to support my family, I had to find a job as soon as possible. Three weeks after I began going to the psychiatrist I started looking around, with his approval. We agreed that it would be best for me to work during regular hours and to avoid any position that might require too much physical output. A few days later I heard about an opening at a rapid treatment center for acute psychiatric patients, operated by the State of Ohio at the Summit County Receiving Hospital in Cuyahoga Falls. When I talked with the superintendent, I told him that I used narcotics periodically to relieve my pain, but glossed over the fact that it had created an addiction problem. I explained that I had worked in the Maine State Hospital, and I used the superintendent there as a reference. Whatever he told the man in Cuyahoga Falls about me couldn't have been bad, because I was hired a few days after I applied for the job.

At that time, Ohio had an excellent concentrated instruction program for general practitioners who were entering psychiatric work. With the state paying me a salary commensurate with what I would receive after my training, I studied at the Cleveland Psychiatric Institute, working from 8:00 A.M. to 6:00 P.M. daily for three months. The program included lectures, ward work, practical treatment of patients with staff psychiatrists, and assisting with experimental therapy. I then returned to the Summit County Receiving Hospital, where I worked as a student under the clinical director in an absorbing in-training program. We covered just about all types of psychiatric treatment, including, among other things, the administration of electric-shock and insulin-coma therapy. At the end of six months, I was put in charge of half the hospital's male patients.

I enjoyed this work more than any I had done in the field of medicine up to that time. Since this was a rapid treatment program, each hospital psychiatrist had his own psychologist and his own social worker, to whom he could assign patients after releasing them from the hospital. By getting these people out as rapidly as possible, I could be sure that my patient load was rarely over twenty men. The rapid treatment policy permitted us to keep a patient no longer than 120 days. At the end of that time we had to either have him well enough so that he might return to society or, if this were impossible, to send him to a regular state mental institution. Because we could devote so much time to each patient, our results were quite good. We sent about 85 percent back to their homes and into productive jobs.

I worked hard, had much success, and was regarded highly at the hospital. Besides treating my own patients, I administered all the shock therapy needed by any special-risk patient. Because of my training in anesthesiology, I was the first staff member to handle a new technique that required the administration of muscle-relaxant drugs along with the Pentothal used to put shock-therapy patients to sleep before applying the shock itself. These relaxants anesthetize the nerve endings and lessen the severity of muscle seizure, but must be given very carefully because the combination of relaxants and electric shock can cause depression of the respiratory center, and respiratory arrest beyond the safety limit of about a minute might follow. This rarely happens, but in case it does the presence of a trained anesthesiologist is essential. He immediately recognizes the danger of overlong respiratory arrest, and knows when to slip an endotracheal tube down the windpipe to allow oxygen to reach the brain before there is any permanent damage.

Perhaps because I had been a patient so often myself, I had great empathy with those at the treatment center. My own experience with drugs enabled me to talk to addicts, of which we usually had several, on their own level because I knew that the feelings that each one thought were peculiar to himself were normal for any addict. I never admitted my own addiction, but my patients realized that I knew a great deal more about their problems than the average doctor might.

Any good doctor has confidence in himself and his own theories on how to handle patients. The longer I remained on the treatment center staff, the more convinced I became that a doctor's kindness, understanding, patience, and, above all, real interest (shown by frequent personal contact with those under his care), are essential to the success of his treatment. Without these ingredients, shock therapy and medication may be wasted except in the mildest of cases.

While you can't change the thoughts of a psychotic patient, you can sometimes relieve pressures upon him by changing his external environment. Even when violence or threats of violence present a danger, I think that for every fatal blowup there could be a thousand happy endings. The only reason there aren't is that too many patients of this type are treated as criminals rather than as victims of illness.

I treated a schizophrenic from Akron, who had been a football teammate of mine in high school. He was admitted to the hospital because he tried to strangle his wife. Although he did have a psychiatric record, he possessed no criminal record, and this was the first time he had ever threatened to harm anybody. During the period when I had him under treatment in the hospital, I let him go home several weekends. When he seemed to be doing well we let him stay home for about a month before the time we would normally have discharged him, asking him to report back to us twice a week. Not long after he was released, I received a 2:00 A.M. phone call from his wife, who told me that he had a gun, threatened to kill her, then went to a vacant furnished apartment in the same building, where he announced that he would kill the first person who entered. Since the apartment was a twin to their own, she gave me its exact layout, and immediately after hanging up I got into my car and drove to Akron, about three miles from where I lived. On the way, I stopped at the nearest police station, explained the problem, and suggested that I might be able to talk this man out of using his gun, because of our old friendship and the fact that he had been under my care. Two officers then followed me in a police car, and we met in front of the man's home.

There was a long hallway leading to the door of the apartment he was in. With the policemen far enough behind me to be invisible, I rapped on the door.

"Who is it?" he yelled.

"Jim DeWitt."

"Stay out, Jim. I'll kill the first person who walks in and I don't want it to be you."

"Have I ever done anything to hurt you, Bill? Haven't I always tried to help you?"

"That doesn't matter. Nobody's going to take me and lock me up."

"Nobody intends to. All I want to do is talk to you."

After a few moments of silence, during which I wondered just how smart I'd be to walk in on an armed psychotic, he mumbled something I couldn't understand. It sounded conciliatory, though, so I said, "Bill, I'm coming in."

Again he mumbled incoherently, and I decided to take a chance. Although a psychotic will usually carry out a threat, this man had stopped threatening, and now I was sure that he wanted to talk to me. The door was unlocked, and I let myself into the sparsely-furnished apartment. Bill was sitting on a chair, his face a picture of dejection. Across his lap lay a rifle, which he did not touch as I approached him.

"What's bugging you, Bill?" I asked softly.

"My wife."

"That's what happened the last time." As I talked, I carefully pulled up a chair and sat beside him as he watched me closely. "She got you going, and you landed in the hospital. Why don't we see if we can clear this up by talking it out?"

"Did my wife call you?"

"Yes. She was frightened, Bill." I paused, then said, "I'll shoot straight with you, the way I always have. I brought two cops with me, but I'll tell them to leave if there isn't any trouble."

He sighed. "There won't be, Jim."

I went down the hall and told the officers everything was all right, that I was taking him back to the hospital. One eyed my huge frame and said, "Okay, doc. You look as if you can take care of yourself." Then they both left.

As I re-entered the apartment, Bill was in the process of emptying the clip from the rifle. I watched him as he stood it up in a closet, then came back and sat down. I sat beside him and asked, "Bill, do you hate your wife?"

"I love her, Jim. I don't know what gets into me."

"Nothing so serious that it can't be straightened out," I said. "Come on back to the hospital with me. I'll put you in an open ward because I trust you. While you're there, we'll work things out."

He followed quietly as I walked down the hall, then got into the front seat while I slid under the wheel. After stopping downtown for doughnuts and coffee in an all-night joint, we went to the hospital and I admitted him to the open ward. I saw him every day, not for long periods, but long enough to assure him that I hadn't lost interest in him. After a couple of weeks, during which I learned from his wife that she wanted him back, I let him go home again. This was a calculated risk, but the kind I think a psychiatrist must take when it seems warranted, just as when I walked into the apartment.

He had already threatened to kill his wife twice. A third threat—and tragedy—was possible. Paranoid reactions of this type are often directed at only one person, who in this case was the patient's wife. However, she didn't want to leave him, and I felt that they could iron things out between them.

I was wrong, but not dangerously so. Bill didn't threaten to kill his wife again, but he suddenly had her committed to a mental institution, convincing the clerk of courts that there was something wrong with her. We got her out in three days and found Bill a job with Goodwill Industries. At a conference involving all parties, we decided to move these people out of the apartment where they had had so much trouble. We found them a place in a different part of town, and about a year after his release, I learned that they were getting along fine.

After working for nearly a year at the treatment center, I was allowed to take on private patients, and received more referrals than I could handle. Now making a good living, enjoying my hospital job, and handling additional patients of my own, I should have been happy and confident of my future. Instead, as the months passed, I began falling into fits of depression, at first mild but later so intense that I couldn't sleep. Free of drugs for more than two years, I made a typical junkie's mistake: thinking I was cured, I began taking something before going to bed. I started with one Seconal or Nembutal a night, soon doubled the dosage, doubled it again, and eventually took so much that, instead of relaxing me, the pills only upset me. This, too, is typical. The more upset an addict becomes, the more he takes of the upsetting agent. In trying to get rid of the upset, he finds himself on the same old vicious merry-go-round. Before moving on to the next step, narcotics, I realized, when I couldn't get up to go to work, that I needed help. After a talk with my psychiatrist in Cleveland, I agreed to go to a private hospital. In a few weeks he pulled me out of what had threatened to become another disastrous bout with drugs.

I returned to the rapid treatment center, where the superintendent, a most understanding man who had probably known more about me originally than I thought he had, welcomed me back on the staff. I functioned normally for about four weeks, but I knew something was wrong. To begin with, I had lost confidence in myself, and a doctor without self-confidence is like a car without an engine. Besides that, I was full of remorse, self-pity, and self-condemnation, wondering what right I had to treat patients no worse off than I.

To top everything off, Kay was acting peculiarly. I don't think she ever accepted my apparent rehabilitation as such, for she continued to be cold and unresponsive. She began withdrawing further and further into herself, sometimes spending long hours in our semi-dark basement, staring at nothing, while refusing to do even the simplest household chores. Under any circumstances I would have wanted her to seek help, and her own psychiatric history made such a move especially essential in my opinion. Her reaction, when I suggested this to her was violently negative, and she was soon downgrading me even more intensely than I had downgraded myself. She quoted a national magazine article that stated that men addicted to anything were spineless and lacked the guts to accept responsibility. She accused me of neglecting my duties as a father, which wasn't true, since the less Kay did for the children the more I took over. She also insisted that I was contemplating leaving her, which wasn't true either.

The combination of my own feelings of inadequacy and Kay's actions built up new anxieties, which once again led to sleeping pills for me. I started with Doriden. This is not a barbiturate and at that time was thought to be a safe, non-habit-forming synthetic drug. In fact, it was just the opposite, and soon I snowballed rapidly to two, three, four a night, in addition to several every two or three hours during the day. Once again my work folded, as I failed to show up at the hospital and cancelled appointments with my private patients while I stayed in bed. I told my wife it was because of back and leg pains, but she knew that I was on something. Actually, I was on whatever nonnarcotic I could get—Doriden, Seconal, phenobarbital—in pill form.

One night I suffered a grand mal seizure. I remember the way it came on. I woke up at about 3:00 A.M. with tremendous anxieties and fears, then lost consciousness and had such a violent convulsion that I landed on the floor. Kay called Don Powers, our minister, and he arrived just after I came to my senses after having been unconscious ten or fifteen minutes. I stood up, turned on the light and saw that my mouth was bleeding; I had bitten my tongue. The seizure, similar to an epileptic fit, was the first one I had ever suffered.

Don suggested that I call my psychiatrist in Cleveland, which I did, and he told me to get some Dilantin, an anti-convulsive drug, right away. I phoned an all-night pharmacy in Akron, and Don drove down and picked up the medication for me. I took two capsules. Then, physically exhausted from the convulsion and mentally depressed, I finally got to sleep at about 5:00 A.M. The next day I shot some Demerol, which started me on a cycle of sleeping and shooting, sleeping and shooting, hour after hour. When I fell out of bed that night and couldn't get up, Kay called an internist who had been treating me for pain from time to time.

I woke up the next morning in the same mental ward where I worked, surrounded by my own patients. One asked me if he could go home that week, and I told him I didn't know because I wasn't his doctor anymore. A couple of others asked me what had happened, but I had no explanation. The one who wanted to go home kept pestering me about it; he was clearly out of orbit, without the least bit of understanding that I was now there as a fellow patient, not a doctor. The whole business of being a patient among former patients was obviously very difficult for me, especially when relatives came during visiting hours and asked me how their kin in the ward were getting along. Eventually, when they realized that I was there myself under a 90-day commitment, they kept staring at me and wondering what had happened. Since there was no place to hide, I couldn't do anything but sit and take it.

The people suffering the most from my fall from grace were my parents. This was my home town and theirs, the place where my father had been first principal of the high school, then superintendent of schools, then supervisor of secondary education. This was the place in which a new school building had been named after him. This was the place where he knew practically everybody, and practically everybody, including hospital staff members and many patients and their relatives, knew him. He was one of the most respected men in town, and I had stigmatized him as the father of a drug addict, of a doctor who couldn't control his own problems, let alone help others to control theirs.

Kay, who seemed to come out of her depression when I was committed, came to see me occasionally, but only to tell me that this was the last chance she was going to give me. I vowed that if I ever got out of there I'd never take drugs again, but the first day that I was given ground privileges, I walked to a nearby drug store and bought a nonbarbiturate relaxant. Back at the hospital, I took one, then another, then so many more that I lost my head. Although I don't remember it, I was later told that I walked to the nurses' station and began to speak incoherently.

The next morning the psychiatrist in charge of me told me

that only long-term commitment to the state hospital would help me break the habit pattern of using drugs as an escape. I tried to talk him out of it, but he was adamant and suggested a two-year commitment. Even retrospectively, I can see that this was a sign of his poor judgment based upon frustration and ignorance concerning the disease of drug dependency. His misconception of proper treatment was almost universal at that time, and is far too widespread even now. Long-term hospitalization actually does nothing for addicts—and, in fact, can do serious harm. What counts is their treatment, the way they are handled, the empathy of their doctors, the fact that their hospitalization removes them from temptation. I have always believed this, not only with respect to addicts but to all mental patients.

In spite of my pleading and arguing, I was transferred from the receiving hospital in Cuyahoga Falls to the Apple Creek State Hospital, near Akron. The transfer was made in writing, with a recommendation by both the psychiatrist and the receiving hospital superintendent that I remain at Apple Creek for two years. An actual commitment was unnecessary, since the receiving hospital was part of the state mental hospital system and I had already been committed.

The next three weeks were a nightmare of discomfort and anxiety. I was in the admission ward, a typical old state hospital ward with scarred, beaten-up floors, barred doors and windows, and too many people. The place was so crowded that the only way I could get into bed was to crawl in from the foot, since the cots practically touched each other. Most of the patients were out of touch with reality and, as always in state hospitals, I had the feeling that I was living in Dante's *Inferno*. People paced, rocked, screamed, babbled incoherently, or simply lay down and stared vacantly, living in worlds of their own, thinking of God only knows what.

My psychiatrist was a good man, but desperately overworked. It would have taken a staff of twenty top-grade psychiatrists to even make a dent in this dreadful, depressing place. Whenever we talked—which was three or four times during that three-week period—I tried to make him understand that this place was doing me no good and never would if I stayed a week, a month, a year, or two years. He disagreed. Before a final decision would be made, I would have a chance to plead my case before a board some time before my original 90-day commitment was up, which meant within the next month.

I went over questions that I thought would be asked, and answers I could give that might sway the board from the two-year commitment I knew was being recommended for me, but I had little hope of success. I knew I was at the mercy of the board; these people could do whatever they chose with me. I also knew that the recommendations of doctors or superintendents who had worked with the patient were nearly always accepted in these hearings, and that whatever I said would have little, if any, effect upon the board members. I steeled myself for the confrontation by giving myself repeated pep talks to act naturally, not to lose my head, and to present my arguments logically and without rancor.

I was given 24 hours' notice of my pending appearance, which came five days before my 90-day commitment ended. I lay awake the entire previous night, trying again to anticipate all possible questions and all possible answers. By morning, I was certain I had covered every angle. Nervous, anxious, depressed, and upset, I was still determined to put forth the appearance of being confident and relaxed when I went before the board.

Seven or eight psychiatrists, all holding copies of my history of addiction and the psychological examinations I had undergone at various hospitals, were sitting at a long table in a conference room. My doctor escorted me in and introduced me to the hospital superintendent, and I was told to sit in a chair directly opposite him at the table. The superintendent briefly went over my recent history, and stated, for the benefit of the other doctors, that I had had a long-term drug addiction problem.

I sat quietly, answering questions, most of which had to do with my own feelings about a long-term commitment—to which, of course, I was opposed. They also asked me what I would do if released, whether I thought I could continue the practice of medicine or, if not, what else I might do. The interview was discouraging, and there was little I could say except that prolonged hospitalization would do me no good and my family considerable harm. I said I could function outside the hospital and would give up medical practice if they thought it advisable. Finally, the superintendent thanked me and said I would be informed of the decision.

I left the room knowing no more than when I had gone in, except that I didn't think I had made much of an impression upon these men, whose minds, I felt, had been made up before they saw me. I heard nothing the following day. When the psychiatrist came around, he paid no attention to me, although I continually called his name. However, the second day after the hearing, the superintendent entered the nurses' station, and a nurse came out to tell me that he wanted to see me.

As soon as I sat down, he said, "The psychiatrists felt that you should be here on a two-year commitment, but I don't agree with them. I believe, as you do, that the length of the hospital stay has no bearing upon a case such as yours. Therefore, we are releasing you in three days, at the end of your original commitment period."

Surprised and delighted, I called Kay, telling her when to come for me. Without seeming unfriendly, she told me she doubted that she could get to the hospital because of the kids, but offered to ask someone to pick me up. Don Powers later phoned and said he would come down—a gesture typical of him. No matter how many times I fell on my face, he was always there to try to help me back.

He left me off in the driveway of my house, and as I walked through the garage and started up the steps, happy to be home again, Kay, who had been standing at the kitchen door when we arrived, simply stared at me. When I reached out to embrace and kiss her, she turned her back, went into the living room, and sat down. From then on, she rarely spoke to me, and I can't recall receiving a single affectionate word or gesture from her thereafter. The children, on the other hand, greeted me effusively when they got home from school, all four hugging and kissing me. In the next few weeks we all—minus Kay—had a wonderful time together. I took them on long rides to the country, where we hiked through woods and out to a swamp, talking about birds, mammals, fish, and other creatures of the outdoors. They asked innumerable questions, but not once did any of them refer to my most recent hospitalization.

Two or three days after arriving home, I decided I had to make some public appearance, because sooner or later it would be necessary for me to face the neighbors. So I mowed the lawn. Using a power mower, I hit every corner, ending up, as I always did, with piles of grass on the cement ramp leading to the garage. A few neighbors waved—and while waving back I realized that they were prepared to act as if nothing had happened.

My only problem was myself. Somehow, I couldn't get rid of the terrible feeling of remorse and depression that had now been haunting me for months. Rather than subsiding, it built up as days passed. I couldn't understand that this was a new life for me and that I should be facing the future with confidence instead of apprehension. In my mind I kept dwelling upon the bleak past and looking forward to a future no more encouraging. Inevitably, I slipped back into the old patterns. Remembering, from the days when I was learning hypnosis, that sodium amytal and amphetamines together provided a strong depressive release, which could last as long as 24 hours, I went to a drugstore and bought a dozen seven-and-a-half-grain sodium amytal ampules. I emptied an ampule shot in 5 cc's of sterile water to dissolve the crystals, drew the mixture into the syringe, then drew up 1 cc (20 mgs) of amphetamines into the solution. I put my blood pressure cuff on my left arm, pumped it up to "tie off" the blood vessels, inserted the needle in a vein, released the pressure, and shot the mixture intravenously. That caused a warm, tingling sensation that suddenly exploded in the center of my abdomen, then slowly spread to my entire body and mind. This lasted for an hour or so, then slowly was replaced by the same type of depression that had caused me to shoot in the first place.

I continued to shoot, with the warmth and glow lasting for shorter and shorter periods, to be replaced by deeper and deeper depressions. When the ampules were gone, I bought more, and within a week was completely hooked again. The turning point this time came when I shot in the basement and woke up on the living room floor. I have no idea how I got there and whether or not Kay saw me. All I know is that nobody was home when I came to my senses.

When I stood up, I suddenly realized that I was riding along that same road, which could lead only to hell. I remembered a former patient whom I had treated for acute depression. In the course of our talks, he had told me that he was an alcoholic who, by trying to live the simple steps of Alcoholics Anonymous, had been able to stay sober for about six years. Now I called him and told him my problem, and he got me admitted to the alcoholic ward of the St. Thomas Hospital in Akron. Aside from the incidents in Boston and Washington, I had had no compulsive desire for liquor. Although I had once admitted to being an alcoholic, I now wasn't so sure, but felt that if AA worked for alcoholics perhaps it would work for drug addicts, too.

However, since my friend, after picking me up and taking me to the hospital, had had to sign me in as an alcoholic, I was given an alcoholic's treatment. This included a mixture of alcohol and chloral hydrate four times a day, which, while it usually calmed an alcoholic, did just the opposite for me: I paced the floor, my nerves in a frazzle. Finally, my sponsor was called in to help me. By talking constantly about anything that came into his head, he kept me from walking out of the ward, a small, neat room with only about eight beds. At his suggestion, the doctor, a nun, took me off the alcoholic medication, and I went through my withdrawal from drugs cold turkey.

Altogether, I was hospitalized about six days. The night before I left I attended an AA meeting. The next day, one of the St. Thomas doctors, himself an alcoholic, drove me home, and on the following night took me to an AA meeting in Cleveland. I threw myself completely into the AA program. Only one of the twelve AA steps mentions alcohol—most apply to just plain living. I had hoped to interest Kay in the program because I felt that her participation would be helpful—AA works hard to get the cooperation of members of an alcoholic's family—but Kay would have no part of it. The whole idea of my being an alcoholic as well as a drug addict was abhorrent to her. Whether or not I was an alcoholic, my identification with AA certainly implied it, and in retrospect I realize she didn't even want *me* to go to meetings, let alone attend any herself.

Because our finances had sunk to a serious low, Kay got a part-time job, and from then on seemed more withdrawn than ever. At home, she paid little attention to any of us, and once again I found myself trying to take care of the children singlehandedly. My mother took over the mechanical work of getting them fed, dressed, and off to school in the morning, while I cooked supper and kept the kids occupied at night and on weekends. They all bathed at once—the girls in a tub upstairs, the boys under a shower in the basement.

One day I noticed that Doug, then six, seemed to have lost weight, and a day or so later that he was drinking an inordinate amount of water. While he didn't complain, I thought he had developed a nervous pattern, possible because of my frequent illnesses and absences from home. I began watching him more closely, and became especially concerned about the amount of water he drank—one night between 6:00 and 9:00, his bedtime, I counted nineteen glasses. The next morning I phoned a pediatrician in town and told him that I was sure my son had diabetes, but preferred to have another doctor run a urinalysis on him. A check proved my diagnosis correct, and Doug was hospitalized for about three weeks.

In the meantime, one of my AA doctor friends told me

there was an opening as Director of Medical Services for the city of Akron, for which he felt I was qualified. The work consisted of supervising various clinics and making public health decisions, neither of them physically strenuous duties. The job required only medical experience, of which I now had a great deal.

The toughest part for me was applying for the job, which meant walking in cold on the city's Director of Public Health and presenting my credentials. Normally, this would have been a simple matter, but I had to break down barriers of my own, since this meant another return to society after a comparatively long absence. The first time I tried, I went downtown, drove into a parking lot near the City Building, paid the lot attendant, got out of the car, locked the door— then, without taking a step, unlocked it, got back in, and drove home. I simply could not face the man or answer the questions that I feared he would ask.

When I told Kay that I was going back the next day, she said, "How can you go in tomorrow when you couldn't today?" She had become so accustomed to my feelings of defeat that she didn't believe I could do anything requiring moral courage. As it happened, she was right that time. I drove into town again and after parking and locking the car, went to the City Building, took the elevator to the sixth floor, got off, hesitated, then pushed the "down" button and went back home.

"I knew you wouldn't," said Kay.

"Tomorrow," I said.

"I'll believe it when I see it."

And the next day I made it. Although I might have been partly motivated by anger at Kay's negative attitude, I really wanted the job and was sure I could handle it. The Public Health Director was a kind, thoroughly understanding man.

He knew about me, knew what I had done and where I had been, and must have known that I wasn't a good risk, yet he didn't ask a single embarrassing question. We spoke only of the job and whether or not I would enjoy the work. He helped me fill out the necessary papers, including civil service blanks, and called me a few days later to tell me that I was hired.

My office was near the hospital where Doug was staying, so I saw him at least three times a day. The little fellow took his ailment and the inconveniences that go with it much more philosophically than I did. I was worried about the daily urinalyses, the shots, the dietary restrictions, and everything else a diabetic youngster must contend with, but I could have spared myself the anxiety. Doug wasn't home long before he was handling everything himself, even phoning me to ask whether he could eat something about which he was doubtful.

During Doug's entire hospitalization, I don't think Kay went to see him once, although this wasn't entirely her fault. One of her major problems had always been an aversion to illness in others. She would never walk into a sickroom unless it was absolutely necessary, and this attitude intensified as she continued to withdraw into herself.

Now burdened with my new job, watching and helping Doug in the early stages of his diabetes, and doing what I could for him and the other children, I had my hands full. I think I could have coped with it all if Kay had shown some signs of cooperation. Knowing my history, she should have at least tried to react positively to the attempts of my AA friends' wives to draw her into their circle. Repeatedly, they invited her to various functions, phoned her to see how she was, dropped in to say "hello" and to try to pull her out of her depression, but she repulsed them at every turn. I put up with this as long as I could, but it was a situation I couldn't tolerate forever, especially when Kay began blaming me for Doug's diabetes. I started to escape in my usual manner, but this time my bout lasted a very short time.

After three nights without sleep, I took one three-grain capsule of Amytal, which helped a little, but not enough. The back and leg pains, which had not been the cause of my previous drug experience, intensified during the next two days, and an additional Amytal capsule didn't help. About the third or fourth night after I had taken the first capsule, I blew apart. First one capsule, then two an hour later, then three half an hour after that. When I still couldn't sleep, I drove downtown and got 2 cc's of Demerol. When even that failed to help me sleep, I felt the only answer was a massive dose.

It was morning by then, and, not daring to drive the car, I walked about a mile to a shopping center, where I wrote a prescription for 30 cc's of Demerol, which I had filled and took home. By the time I arrived, Kay, who apparently had received a call from the pharmacist, asked me what I was doing with the drugs. Without answering, I went upstairs, locked myself in the bathroom, and took a hefty shot. While I was there, Don Powers and four other guys arrived, and I have a vague recollection of their banging on the bathroom door, begging me not to shoot.

I passed out. The next thing I knew, I woke up in the city jail, the same one where I had been visiting prisoners in connection with my job. Wearing a black and red plaid shirt with a long rip in front, I was alone in a cell. Realizing that I must have put up a fight, I prayed that I hadn't hurt anyone, especially since all five of the men who had pulled me out of the bathroom before I could kill myself with an overdose were my good friends. I would never have known how much

Demerol I shot, except that there were still 15 cc's left, so I must have given myself the other 15 at one time, enough to knock out anyone unless he had built up to that amount over a fairly long period.

I didn't know why I was sent to jail instead of a hospital, and I never asked. All I know is that when I asked Don if I had hurt anyone, he laughed and said, "You were out like a light. You couldn't have hurt a flea." But I didn't see Don or anyone else except cops and jailers for over a week. I wasn't allowed to have visitors, and was kept under maximum security guard. And, while it was normal procedure to transfer a prisoner from the city jail to the county prison after 24 hours, I never left the city jail. This, I later learned, was because I was a city employee and they wanted the incident kept as quiet as possible—in fact, it never got into the newspapers.

My most vivid memory of the eight days I spent in jail was going into the lineup—a horrible feeling, because it is exactly as depicted in movies and on television. All the men arrested the previous day are brought into a room, with lights shining in their eyes. Each is given a number—mine was six—and when his number is called, each identifies himself by name, is asked if he knows the charge, answers in whichever way he chooses, and is then questioned. From everything I had heard and read, I gathered that a police lineup is usually for identification purposes, with strangers lining up along with the suspect, who may then be picked out by witnesses to his crime, if any. In my lineup, however, all the prisoners apparently had been caught in the act, and there was no need for identification. Anyone who may have been in the audience—which none of us could see, because of the bright lights—must have been there as interested parties. If any were my friends, I didn't know it.

When they called the number six, I said, "James C. De-Witt," leaving out my medical title.

"Do you know what you are charged with?" an officer asked.

"Writing a false prescription," I said.

"Narcotics?"

"Yes."

That was the end of my questioning. Later, I went with the other prisoners into the exercise yard, and still later I was taken to be mugged and fingerprinted by officers I knew, one of whom said, "Hi, doc, how ya doing?"

"Not so good, I guess," I said.

A kid of about 21, who had been charged in the lineup with attempted murder, came up to me back in the exercise yard and said, his eyes gleaming in apparent admiration, "Hey, buddy, you booked on narcotics?"

"Yes."

"Gee, you're big!"

I didn't feel very big. I wanted to be so small that I could crawl into a hole and disappear. I was, as always, ashamed, remorseful, utterly desolate. Once again, I had let down my family, including my highly respected father and my diabetic son, and this time it had happened so quickly that I didn't even suffer withdrawal pains. I couldn't understand it, and didn't want to face it.

After eight days I was released on $3,000 bail, put up by my father. One of my AA buddies picked me up and said, "Jim, I'm going to take you home with me for a few days. You and my brother will have a good time because he's home from medical school and has been looking forward to meeting you."

I stayed with him for several days because he was afraid that if I went home I'd fall right back into the same old pattern. After I had been there nearly a week, the City Director of Public Health called and said, "Jim, when you're up to it, we want you back. I've talked it over with the mayor and it's all right with him."

"After what I've done, you want me back?"

"You're a fine doctor, Jim. We know your problem. There's no reason for it to cost you your job."

Amazed and delighted, I thanked him and told him I'd be back as soon as I could. Then my host phoned my wife to tell her that the city officials were letting me keep my job and that he was taking me home the next day.

When I arrived, I walked into a frigid household. Kay was there alone, and the minute I arrived she went down to the basement. When the kids returned from school, they gave me the same wonderful, warm greeting they always had. I took them all to a hamburger place for dinner, and we had a happy reunion.

The breach between Kay and me widened in the next few weeks, during which I remained clean of drugs. She only spoke to me to re-emphasize her disgust with me and to tell me that with my addiction, my AA activities, and my general behavior, I was driving her crazy. She began speaking about leaving, and spending virtually all her time in the basement, where she sometimes listened to a portable radio or read a book by a dim light. She usually stayed down there until about 1:00 A.M. I always waited up for her, but she never had anything to say and we never made love, although we continued to share the same bed.

I didn't mind her attitude toward me—indeed, considering the hardship to which I had subjected her for so many years, I could hardly blame her—but I was upset about her indifference to the children and angry that she was slowly developing a venomous hatred for my father. This gentle man had done so much for us all, and had been so patient throughout our troubles, that I didn't see how he could be blamed for anything. I guess the simple fact that he was my father was all that Kay needed. She baited him, insulted him, snubbed him, and conversed with him as little as possible.

By the time Doug was out of the hospital, he and the other children were spending more time with my parents than with us. Julie, the baby, actually lived with them. The others were always there for breakfast and left for school from there. At night, the kids often went with me, even accompanying me to the city jail when I resumed my visits to check on the health of the prisoners.

One afternoon, when my father stopped by to see the children, Kay said, "I think I'll get out."

For one of the very few times in his life Dad, who rarely snapped at anyone no matter how annoyed he was, came close to blowing his stack.

"Why don't you quit talking about it and just shove off?" he shouted.

When I came home the next day, she was gone.

IX

K AY was away for about two months. I later learned that she had spent part of that time in motels and the rest in a sanitarium, and had never ventured far from Akron. In her absence, Julie continued to live with my parents, and the older children stayed with me six nights a week, joining my mother and father the one night I attended AA meetings. Although I had help from my mother, my daily routine was busy, strenuous, and hardly suitable for a drug addict inclined to seek escape from his self-induced problems even under the best of conditions. Under a strain such as this, I was never certain when I might return to this form of escape. Perhaps my many responsibilities, plus the pleasure of spending so much time with the children, kept me off drugs while Kay was gone—although, heaven knows, there might have been some excuse for almost anything I did to ease my anxieties. I got the kids ready for bed every night, did what I could to keep the house presentable, prepared breakfast, checked Doug's urinalysis and insulin (although he took care of it himself, I always checked it when I was home), and after breakfast took all three children to my mother's. She packed their lunches and sent them off to school while I went to work. We usually had dinner at her house, although I sometimes took the kids out to eat. We always did something together in the evening, even if it was only a matter of their accompanying me on my nightly rounds, including my regular visits to the jail.

My first indication that Kay was about to return came when my lawyer called me. When I met him for lunch (his office was only half a block from mine) he told me that Kay's lawyer had phoned to tell him that she wanted a legal separation and that the four of us were to meet the next evening at her lawyer's office. When I learned that Kay's lawyer was a friend and frequent colleague of mine on church committees, I anticipated few problems. I didn't realize that the facts of law don't always coincide with the facts of human relationships. You can't think of an opposing lawyer as a friend; he must, by the very nature of his profession, be your foe, just as your own lawyer, even if only a casual acquaintance, must be your ally. My only previous brushes with the law had been through cops and narcotics agents. This was my first experience with a civil action.

Kay was the last to appear at the meeting. She said a flat "Hi," and after she sat down her lawyer announced that she was suing for divorce. He read the charges against me: gross neglect of duty, extreme cruelty, and nonsupport. There was no mention of drugs. When I asked for an explanation of the charges, her lawyer said that they were standard procedure. I then remarked that, under the conditions that existed at the time—with me taking care of the children and doing my best to support the family when I was physically able—it wouldn't be easy to make those charges stand up in court.

"If you want to buck me on any of these charges, I'll put in some real ones," he said. "I've got a whole drawer full of them, and I'll get as tough as I have to."

I had no choice but to back down, since the narcotics charge against me was still pending, and my long record as a drug user spoke for itself. A hearing was scheduled before a court referee, and, at the request of my lawyer, I wrote up eight or ten pages on Kay's psychiatric history, which predated the beginning of my addiction by many years. However, when I realized that the combination of my addiction and her emotional instability might show neither of us as a suitable parent and possibly cause the children to be separated and placed in foster homes, I refused to let my lawyer present my paper on Kay to the referee. When I saw Kay just before the hearing, I said, "Why don't you drop this? We can work something out so the kids won't get hurt."

"Just being around you is hurting them enough," she replied.

Despite her hostile attitude, I felt it would be better for her to win custody than for the children to fall into the hands of the court, so I persisted in my refusal to use the paper I had written. I told my lawyer not to contest the charges. Kay was granted temporary custody of the children, and I was ordered to leave the house by 5:00 the next afternoon. I had visitation rights for one hour two evenings a week, and for Saturday or Sunday from 10:00 A.M. to 5:00 P.M.

I moved in with my parents the day after the hearing. The children were terribly upset when I told them that I was leaving the next day, that their mother and I were temporarily separating, and that my visits with them would be limited, but I assured them that everything would eventually work out. Naturally, I was whistling in the dark. Although I clung to a forlorn hope that Kay might change her mind for the sake of the children, I knew in my heart that we would never get together again. I also knew that now it was only a matter of time before I would resume the drug pattern, because my visits with the kids would tear me apart. And, of course, it was such an ordeal to leave them at a set time whenever we got together that the pressure in me built up to the inevitable point of explosion and collapse.

I lasted about a month and a half, then started taking Miltown at night. I picked it because I thought that, while acting as a tranquilizer, it was least likely to get me into serious trouble. It was also easy to obtain, since a doctor could get it without a prescription. I started with three or four tablets—twice the normal dosage—because I hadn't had a decent night's sleep in weeks. I had never heard of anyone snowballing Miltown, but I snowballed it pretty rapidly. Within a week and a half I was up to 75 tablets a day, taking them a dozen at a time, and actually knocking myself out. When at last I couldn't go to work, I phoned the Veterans Hospital at Brecksville and went in as a voluntary patient. My father drove me there, and after admission I was put into a locked ward as a drug addict.

Never having been hooked on Miltown before, I wasn't sure what to expect or what sort of withdrawal I might have. The orders at the hospital were to withhold medication of any kind, the theory being that the best way to get me off pills was to keep me from taking any. It was pure conjecture and turned out to be erroneous. After about six hours I started to feel electric shocks going through my body, foreshadowing some sort of seizure. The seizure must have followed immediately, because the next thing I remember is waking up alone in a seclusion room off the main ward, with the door open. Since I tasted blood, I knew I had bitten my tongue, so I called an attendant. When he brought in a nurse, I asked her for Dilantin, which, besides arresting seizures, has no sensory effect, changes no emotions, and is non-habit-forming.

The nurse checked, and came back to tell me that her

orders were not to give me anything. I said that I would surely have more seizures, and that there was no way Dilantin could hurt me, but she couldn't contradict her orders. Before I could ask for a doctor, I felt another seizure coming on, and the next 36 hours were a living hell—one petit mal seizure after another, with an occasional grand mal that knocked me out. Sometimes only one arm or one leg was involved, and I didn't lose consciousness as I thrashed around, unable to control the muscle action. At one point I dislocated a shoulder when I banged my arm against the wall. It must have been during a grand mal seizure because I don't remember when it happened.

I couldn't convince anyone that my shoulder was out of place, and not until a doctor came around about twelve hours and several seizures later was anything done about it. He recognized the dislocation immediately, and had me wheeled to the operating room, where a young resident was on duty. The doctor asked if I minded the resident working on my shoulder under his supervision, and I told him to go ahead. However, the resident had never done this type of job before, and he pulled and hauled and twisted without effect, succeeding only in putting me through more agony. Finally, the doctor, realizing that there had been a great deal of muscle spasm because the shoulder had been out of place for so long, finally took over. He gave me Pentothal and corrected the problem, which really was no big deal, since any experienced doctor could have quickly fixed it. The whole episode, though, simply added to my trauma. The convulsions finally ended 36 hours after they began, and I was lucky that they didn't cause permanent brain damage.

I went to Brecksville in November, 1962 and didn't get out until the following May. My whole stay there was a dead loss, but I couldn't blame the staff. Although the doctors and attendants were sympathetic, they knew nothing about drug addiction—I was the only addict there—and labored under the popular misconception that the longer an addict is hospitalized the better off he'll be when he gets out. Even my parents accepted this as gospel, although there was no factual basis for it. Everyone was still experimenting with treatment for addiction and nobody, including myself, really knew anything. As usual, I looked for the miracle cure that wasn't there.

My psychiatrist, a nice guy, used all sorts of technical terms that sounded important but were meaningless. He once told me that all addicts suffered primarily from two definite personality disorders. They were sado-masochists—sadist because they wanted to punish people, masochists because they desired punishment themselves—and their personalities were fixated in the oral stage of development.

"I understand you quite well," I said. "And there are two things I'd like to say. The sado-masochistic tendency shouldn't be difficult to resolve: I'll beat the hell out of you and then you beat the hell out of me. As for the other problem: if you got the cigar out of your mouth when you talked to me, it would be easier for me to see my own oral fixation."

Of course, the whole business was hogwash, and I'm sure he realized it as well as I did, for he replied, "My fixations are socially acceptable and yours aren't." That was the end of the parrying and the therapy.

Before I left the place I was helping the overworked staff as a patient-doctor, a role that by then was quite familiar to me. My entire stay there would have been wasted except for two things—I found it easier to stay off drugs, and, by setting up a medical library at the request of the superintendent, I had a chance to read all the latest information in psychiatric and medical journals.

I left the place with nowhere to go except to my parents' home and nobody really wanting or needing me except my kids, whom I could see only for limited periods. Realizing that there was nothing left for me in Cuyahoga Falls except more frustration, more unhappiness, more grief and more escapes via the drug route, I decided to return to Maine. The impending divorce and the narcotics indictment were still hanging over my head, so I had to get permission to leave Ohio. Having done that, I and my parents drove to Skowhegan, where my sister, Virginia Paul, lived with her husband Bob and their son, and I set up a general practice in nearby Farmington. I replaced a doctor who had left to teach in Boston, taking over his house and office, where I lived alone.

With no other psychiatrist and only one psychologist within many miles of the place, I soon had my hands full. The psychologist, a woman, referred many patients to me, and I did what I could for them. Of course, I was nearly as sick as they were. I missed my children terribly. I received no reply to any letters I sent them or their mother, and could turn to no one for news, since my parents were staying in Skowhegan with my sister for several months after our arrival in Maine.

About all that kept me from going off the deep end again was a doctor friend who lived in Kingfield, Maine, about 30 miles from Farmington, and who loved the outdoors as much as I did. I met him through my sister and her family, who had been patients of his. He and I often went fishing for stripers on the coast at night when the tide was low, and also hunted ducks in the marshes. One of my patients had given me a young pup, which I trained as a hunting dog. When the season began in the autumn, the doctor and I went out for deer, usually leaving from Kingfield—where I spent the night—at about 4:00 A.M. and staying out until about an hour and a half after dawn, at which time we would go our separate ways to handle our practices. This was the only enjoyment I had during the period I spent in Farmington, and it didn't last as long as the hunting season. I couldn't tolerate not seeing my children and not knowing how they were or even where they were.

As my depression deepened, my return to drugs became more imminent. I finally succumbed some time in early October, and soon found it impossible to continue my practice. Realizing that I had to stop somehow, I arranged to spend a weekend at a friend's mountain camp. Late in the evening before I was to leave, exhausted from lack of sleep, I bought two six-packs of beer and spent the night drinking them. When they were finished, I looked in the refrigerator and saw a four-ounce bottle of paraldehyde. Knowing that alcoholics preferred it for withdrawal, I decided to try it, since I had been using booze to get off drugs. It wasn't very smart thinking; I had never given it to a patient, and didn't even know the correct dosage. All I remember is taking a couple of tablespoons with fruit juice. The next thing I knew I awoke in a hospital, where a doctor friend told me that my sister and brother-in-law had found me unconscious on the floor, my pulse rate zero and an empty paraldehyde bottle beside me. Two tablespoons are beyond the lethal dosage. I suppose the only reason I survived was that I was too big, or too mean, to die that easily.

My first thought, upon waking up, was to get out, but the nurse told me I had been committed by my hunting pal, and that I couldn't leave. I harbored no resentments. He knew that I was depressed, that I was back on drugs, and had committed me—with the approval of my sister and her family—for my own good. He was justifiably afraid that I'd kill myself, which I came damn near doing.

Unable to find my clothes, I put on my bathrobe and

walked out the front door to get a cab. I didn't need one. Waiting for me on the steps, with an aide in his car, was the sheriff, whom I knew well. His office was right across the street from my house, and we had spent many pleasant hours talking about hunting and the outdoors.

"Jeez, doc," he said, "I feel awful about this, but we got to take you down to the state hospital."

Once in the car, he apologized again as he put handcuffs on me. On the way to Augusta, we talked about everything except my condition. Only as we approached the entrance did he mention it by saying, "Doc, this won't be for long. There's nothing wrong with you." After we were met by an attendant with a wheelchair, he took the cuffs off, I shook hands with him and his deputy, and they quickly turned and headed back to Farmington.

After being admitted, I was placed in solitary confinement. My cell—it was exactly that—had a peephole at the door and one small window covered by a screen cemented to the wall at the opposite end. The only furniture was a low bed and mattress, covered by a rug or sheet—in the dim light I couldn't tell which. There was no plumbing. You had to shout for an attendant if you wanted to go to the bathroom.

I was in terrible physical pain, but the pain in my head was worse—a hollow, hopeless, crying pain because I was alone again, with no way that anyone could help me. I was completely at the mercy of the doctor in charge of me. He would govern my whole life—when I would eat, when I would sleep, when I would be allowed to go anywhere, how long I would stay, what I would do. The commitment was in his hands, for no one outside the hospital had any jurisdiction anymore. Even my doctor friend who had signed my papers couldn't get me out now. My entire fate depended upon the whim of one doctor. If he were kind and understanding, he might give me a break. If he were hard and tough, he could let me rot if he wished.

As these thoughts coursed through my head, the big latch on the door turned, and in came two attendants and the doctor assigned to me. He looked down at the low mattress where I was sitting and said harshly, "Are you James C. DeWitt?"

"That's right."

"Well," he said, "if you don't die of liver failure or convulsions, you'll live to suffer awhile."

Then he turned and walked out, while one of the attendants slammed the door and turned the latch.

I had my answer. I would get no help or understanding from this man. I knew he meant what he said—that if I didn't die I would live to suffer. Thanks to this sadist, much of the suffering I have lived through was in that Maine State Institution in Augusta. There was no court in the land, no judge, no friend, no wife, no relative, no other doctor to wield influence over him. His power was absolute.

When I was in medical school, someone had once pasted up a sticker in the men's washroom that said something about people railroaded into mental hospitals and kept there for years, forgotten by everyone except the hospital personnel, most of whom were so overworked that they no longer cared. I thought of that now, and wondered if it were about to happen to me. I have since been in worse situations, but never more discouraging ones. This man , who held me in the palm of his hand, was a little dictator reveling in the power that some ridiculous law had given him. His smile was a devil's smile; his pleasure lay in making a tantalizing offer and cruelly withdrawing it at the moment the victim reached for it.

After a few days in the cell, I was transferred to a locked

ward. My doctor, always escorted by a couple of husky attendants—for there were patients who sometimes blew up and had to be forcibly restrained—came into the ward every day, but didn't approach me for three weeks. I finally caught up with him by standing near the nurses' station, where he always showed up sooner or later. As he was unlocking the door leading to it, I said, "Doctor, am I going home pretty soon?"

"You shouldn't be here too long," he said.

"What does that mean?"

"Just what I said. I don't think you'll be here too long."

Then he smiled that diabolical smile and let himself into the nurses' station, which was protected by unbreakable glass so that whoever was on duty could keep an eye on the ward without exposing herself to possible harm by entering it.

The doctor who committed me came to see me about ten days after I got there. He felt terrible because, never having committed anyone before, he had assumed that it was as easy to withdraw the commitment as it was to make it.

"Jim, I don't know what to do," he said. "I can commit, but I can't uncommit."

"I know," I said. "The only guy who can do that is the doctor in charge of me, and I honestly think he's a sadist. I don't know how he got this job or how he keeps it, unless it pays so poorly that he's the only man they can get to take it. How long I stay is entirely up to him."

"I'll talk to him," he said. "We've got to get you out of here within the next week. There's still some deer hunting for us to do."

The hospital routine was similar to that of a prison. Breakfast was at 7:00, lunch at 11:30, supper at 4:30. The food was always the same—dry or cooked cereal, buttered toast and coffee for breakfast, and some baked dish, usually hash, and tea for lunch and supper. Sunday was the only time we had meat not mixed with anything. We could smoke four times a day, after every meal and just before bedtime. Since no one was allowed to have matches, we had to depend on an attendant for a light. We smoked when he decided we could. Most of the attendants were pretty good about it, but one or two waited until the last minute before giving us lights, then made us put out our cigarettes after one or two puffs.

The ward consisted of two small rooms for 30 or 40 patients, with sleeping quarters in an adjoining room. During the day there was no place to lie down and no place to walk, not even a long hallway. You could sit, but there was nothing to read, nothing to do but think. I didn't want to think. I wanted to live in a sort of limbo, where nothing happens except the passage of time, but no sane person can live that way. I had no choice but to think, and my thoughts were of the children I couldn't see and the freedom I couldn't have. Except for my parents, my sister and brother-in-law, and my doctor friend, I never had any visitors.

With my withdrawal over, I was on minimal medication. I had some pain in my back and legs—I always had that and still do—but nothing I couldn't tolerate. But my whole life was in the hands of a man who didn't know the meaning of the word "humanitarian," if, indeed, he had ever heard of it.

Two weeks before Christmas, he said, "Jim, you're going to get a hearing at a staff meeting tomorrow morning."

"Wonderful!" I exclaimed. "Will I be released?"

He just smiled, and said, "I'll see you at staff tomorrow."

The next morning, attendants took three of us to another section of the building, and sat us in a waiting room about twelve feet square. When my doctor came in, he stopped in front of me and said, "Jim, I don't know what's wrong with me today. It must be the Christmas spirit that induced me to bring you up here to release you from the hospital."

Then, leaving me with a beautiful sense of warmth and well-being, he went into the staff room. I felt as though a cloud had been lifted. I began planning the resumption of my practice in Farmington, and called my sister to come and get me.

The other two patients were summoned first. One came out, almost yelling, "I made it! I made it!," and I smiled to myself, thinking, *I'll join you soon.* The other came out tearfully, and I felt sorry for him because I knew he hadn't made it.

When my name was called and I walked into the room, my doctor said, "Stand right over there in front of the chairman." I walked over to the chairman—I found out later that he was the assistant superintendent—and he said, "Why is this man here?"

"He's addicted to drugs of every type," my doctor said. "He's got a long history. Everything's been tried on him without success. He's been given all kinds of therapy and all kinds of help, and none has done him any good. His only chance is a long stay in the hospital."

"Is there anything else?" the chairman asked.

"Yes. As you probably know, he's a doctor. He's a disgrace to the medical profession, a disgrace to humanity."

"Anything else?"

After a moment's silence, the chairman looked at me and snapped, "Back to your ward."

Utterly crushed, I turned and slowly walked out, then was escorted to the ward. The next week was a nightmare, caused not so much by the turndown as by the expectation of release that my doctor had deliberately given me. Over and over, I wondered how he could do such a thing. I was still wondering, a week later, when he came over to where I was sitting.

"Jim," he said, "I've got some good news for you. Your parents will be here for Christmas. I think this is the ideal time for you to be released. They can help you set yourself up to start practicing again. I'll let you know the exact day they come. It might be just before Christmas."

Once again my spirits rose. I thanked him and looked forward to the next week. *This time*, I thought, *I'll surely get out. There must have been some mistake before. I just misunderstood him.*

The days inched by, every minute an hour, every hour a week. I could hardly eat or sleep as my mind played the same refrain over and over: *I'm going to get out—I'm going to get out—I'm going to get out.*

On the day before Christmas, an attendant came over and said, "Jim, you've got visitors." He escorted me to the visiting room, and I walked in alone. It was my mother and father, and I was never so happy to see anyone in my life. After we greeted each other, I said, "I'll go back to the ward and get my things packed."

"What for?" my father said.

"I'm going home with you."

"No, you're not," he said, gently. "We just talked to your doctor. He said you were going to be here a long time."

"You can't be serious," I murmured. "He couldn't do this."

"I'm sorry, son. Maybe it's best. We'll be back to see you tomorrow."

Some Christmas, I thought. *That sonofabitch. I hadn't misunderstood him that time. He's sick, sicker than any of us.*

I was awakened at 5:30 Christmas morning, a most

unusual procedure. For a few seconds I hoped it meant the doctor had changed his mind and decided to let me leave, after all. Then I thought I was about to get the sort of gifts soldiers overseas and institution inmates get—candy, toilet articles, cigarettes, odds and ends of that sort. They would have done more harm than good, for I couldn't have endured receiving things from my children just because it was Christmas—not when I couldn't see or be with them.

But the attendant brought no good news or gifts—just an official-looking document. He handed it to me, and I had only to read the first few lines to know what it was. My divorce was official; my wife had permanent custody of the children. I sank down on my cot and looked at the paper that shattered all my hopes for a normal life at home with my family, stared until I could no longer see through the tears that welled up in my eyes.

Then despair and frustration were replaced by cold anger. I didn't care about Kay. From my viewpoint, she was beyond saving. But the children, what would happen to them? *Kay doesn't really want the kids. She just doesn't want me to have them. What kind of life can she—will she—give them? She is neither willing nor able to take care of them. Why has she done this? Why?*

Before that Christmas day of 1963 ended I had another jolt. An hour after breakfast, an attendant handed me a document that looked similar to the first one. Once again, I had only to read a few sentences in order to realize what it was. An Ohio grand jury had indicted me on narcotics charges. That meant that, no matter where I went or what I did, this would be hanging over my head until it was either filed or acted upon in an Ohio court.

I stared at the paper and laughed bitterly. *You think you can hurt me? You think anything can plunge me into deeper misery? First you make me a zombie, subject to the whims of a sadist. Then you hold out freedom and snatch it away just as I reach for it. Then you take my children from me. I don't need this. I've had everything else. This is just a little frosting you've added to my cake. Thank you.*

I tossed the notification of the indictment onto my cot in much the same spirit as a waiter drops a tray after too many of the dishes have already slipped from it and crashed on the floor. My life was already smashed into little pieces. Everything I held dear was gone forever.

Even seeing my parents, who were leaving for home in a few days, had left me cold, although they promised to check and let me know what was happening in Ohio, told me to keep my chin up, and assured me that I wasn't alone. Actually, I don't think they understood what was happening to me. Even my father, as ignorant about the treatment of addicts as anyone else, believed (as so many doctors and so-called experts did) that a long institution stay might cure me. He was also surprised at neither of the blows that had fallen that morning. He knew that Kay was going through with the divorce, and that sooner or later the indictment would be coming.

Much later, I learned that Kay had given up a job she had had at Kent State College and taken all four children to Atlanta, where her sister lived. Caring for them was more than she could handle. Before she was through, she had given up trying. Karen, her fourteen-year-old shoulders heavy with responsibilities she should never have been forced to assume, had run away, and the three younger children had been placed in a small Tennessee orphanage run by a religious sect. But in that mental hellhole in Augusta I knew none of this, and didn't find it out for at least three years.

As the weeks dragged on, life became a little easier for me.

Right after Christmas, I was assigned to an open ward, and shortly after that to the job of cutting meat in the hospital butcher shop. In February, the doctor let me go to my sister's house on weekends, but I had to fight him every inch of the way to get even that much liberty.

On one of those trips, I saw an old AA friend named Arnold Tobin, who, after nearly wrecking his life with booze, had straightened out and remained dry ever since. He told me about an AA rehabilitation center in Peterborough, New Hampshire, which needed a doctor, preferably someone who had been through the mill himself and understood the problems of alcoholics. I met the owners of the place, which was called Riverdale, on one of my weekends off, and they promised to give me the job if I could get out of the hospital. I told my doctor about it, and asked if he would release me. After a few tantalizing weeks, during which he paid no attention to me, he suddenly said I could go. Bob Paul, my brother-in-law, picked me up and took me to Farmington, and the next day to Riverdale.

It was April, 1964. I had been in the Augusta State Hospital for exactly six months.

X

When I reached Riverdale, there were only about a dozen regular patients in the place, along with perhaps another dozen staying for the weekend. Although I knew AA procedures well after my experience in Ohio, I had never seen a sanitarium-type AA arrangement such as this. It was a combination hospital, drying-out center, and vacation spot for alcoholics. Many of those whom I met on my first weekend there had been dry for some years, but continued to go from time to time because they liked it and it helped them stay dry. A few had just arrived and were going through withdrawal, which is as bad for an alcoholic as for a drug addict.

Although for years I had wavered between admitting I was an alcoholic and refusing to face the fact, I could equate alcoholism with drug addiction, as the two have a great deal in common. To an alcoholic, liquor is as addictive a drug as any type of narcotic is to an addict. The only real difference is that a heavy drinker isn't necessarily an alcoholic and often never will be, whereas no one becomes a heavy drug user without developing into an addict. Anyone who can work with alcoholics can work with addicts, and vice versa. By the time I went to Riverdale, I had worked with both, and I felt, as I still do, that the success of the treatment depends as much upon the empathy of the doctor as upon the medication he might prescribe.

One of AA's most effective features is the unlimited opportunities it gives alcoholics to talk about their troubles. They are encouraged to recall their experiences with booze as often as they wish, and to reiterate their resolutions of sobriety whenever the spirit moves them. Talk is always good therapy for the nondrinking alcoholic. Repeated stories of booze problems, which often bore a nonalcoholic after one recital, never bore another alcoholic, who lends a sympathetic ear even when he has heard the same stories over and over again, because listening is as good therapy as talking. This is one reason that AA members tend to seek each other out, especially in the early stages following withdrawal. And this is the principal reason for AA meetings, which follow a fairly consistent pattern. They last anywhere from an hour to an hour and a half, depending upon the area in which they are held, and the speakers are selected in basically the same way everywhere. In Massachusetts, for example, AA meetings last about an hour and a half. Usually three alcoholics stand and relate their stories of where booze took them and what it cost them in terms of money, family relationships, self-respect, etc. They usually tell how the AA program has helped them to regain and maintain their sobriety. This they do by trying to follow the twelve steps of AA on a 24-hour basis. They emphasize that yesterday is a cancelled check and tomorrow a promissory note, if we live to the best of our ability today. The alcoholics who speak at these meetings are usually asked in advance, so that no pressure is put upon a person if he would rather not speak. This spares him the embarrassment of a public refusal.

At Riverdale, there were two AA meetings a week, one of which was Sunday, the day I arrived there. Despite my long association with AA and frequent attendance at AA meetings in Ohio, I had never spoken before any of the groups there, largely because I had doubts about my being an alcoholic. Except for social drinking at parties and my shattering episodes in Boston and Washington, I had never done much heavy drinking. And, as far as I could recall, liquor alone had never gotten me into trouble.

However, since I was the new doctor, the people at Riverdale asked me to tell those at the Sunday AA meeting something about myself. Never having spoken in public before, I was a little nervous, reluctant to bring up the subject of my drug addiction, and unable to recall much about my alcoholic episodes. The result was a brief, dry series of short statements amounting to little more than the fact that, having had some experience in and knowledge of psychiatry, I had treated alcoholics and addicts and hoped that I could help these people. The talk lasted three minutes and 45 seconds, during which I said everything I could think of saying.

As time went on, I gave longer and longer talks, during which I was more specific about the subject of my addiction, but clinical and impersonal about my alcoholism, which I was unwilling to accept. These talks were not confined to AA meetings at Riverdale, for I often spoke elsewhere as Riverdale's doctor. Once, when addressing a large group at an AA anniversary celebration in Farmington, I approached the podium with mixed emotions. The hall in which I spoke was a block from where I had been found unconscious less than a year before.

Although architecturally an old farmhouse, Riverdale was modern in every other respect. The setting was beautifully rustic, the atmosphere relaxed and restful. The couple who ran it, both nondrinking alcoholics, had raised approximately a quarter of a million dollars to reconstruct the place, and had done a remarkable job. On the first floor of this rambling building, there was plush carpeting everywhere except in the office and the infirmary. The dominant feature was a living room about 20 by 40 feet, with large picture windows and a big stone fireplace. The dining room had three large tables, with room for about fifteen people at each and picture windows on two sides overlooking a meadow which extended in a gradual slope down through the woods and to the river that gave the place its name.

The small infirmary, although used almost exclusively for acute withdrawal patients, also had facilities for taking care of minor ailments. It was in a new section that had been added to the original structure. Two adjoining small wards, one with three beds, the other with four, with a nurses' station adjacent to one and a television room adjacent to the other, were cheerful and bright. Barring unforeseen complications following withdrawal, patients rarely stayed more than three or four days. They were then transferred to well-furnished individual rooms, with private bathrooms and all the earmarks of a first-class motel.

My room, one of the nicest there, was in the new section, near the infirmary, and a bit isolated from the rest of the house. By the time I arrived there, practically fresh from my ghastly experience in Augusta, I was in pretty good shape, having had no drugs or liquor for over six months.

A good deal of my work was consultation, not only with patients but with their relatives. In any addictive situation, the person closest to the patient usually needs as much help as the patient himself. Sometimes that relative—wife, husband, grown child, or parent, in most cases—has hangups of his own, accompanied by a natural irritability and impatience with the alcoholic. A close association often precipitates the upset that leads to new problems resulting in resumption of the patient's addiction. By this I don't necessarily mean that the relative has caused the original addiction—only its continuation. If the relative can establish the proper attitude of understanding, the chances of the patient's permanent abstinence are that much greater. This is the type of therapy that would have helped me in the early stages of my own addiction. Although I certainly couldn't hold anything against Kay, a better understanding on her part might have helped as my addiction progressed. Her attitude of disgust was not unusual. I found several cases of alcoholics' relatives with the same attitude. However, the very fact that they came to Riverdale was a good sign, for at least it meant that they wanted help, for both themselves and their loved ones. Often, the patient recovered faster than the relative. The doctor, in this case me, had to be a combination medical man, father confessor, and supporting shoulder for all parties concerned. This is why I believe that a doctor who has been through these problems himself is more likely to do some good than one who hasn't, although I have seen plenty of effective doctors with no personal history of either alcoholism or addiction.

After being settled in my quarters in Riverdale, I was taken to the basement under the new section of the house, which was actually a large recreation room with billiard, ping pong, and card tables, lounges, and a television. A large coffee urn was continually working (wherever addicts of any type are treated, there should always be coffee—a good, harmless substitute for drugs or liquor), and there were plenty of doughnuts on a huge platter. Several coffee tables were scattered about the room, and I sat at one with an attendant—an alcoholic, like most of the staff personnel.

Shortly after we were seated, we were joined by a tall, attractive nurse with light blue eyes and gray-streaked brown hair. Her name was Doris Drew; she was an Irish Catholic from Lowell, Massachusetts, separated from her husband, who, because of her alcoholism, had custody of her two children. She had recently recovered from a booze bout of her own, and was paying her fee by working as a nurse, a job at which she was very competent.

We all talked at some length, but I don't recall many details of our conversation. I do remember being attracted to this woman. Despite the streaks of gray hair, she was only in her late twenties or early thirties, and she told me later that her hair had begun to turn gray while she was in her teens. She was a bubbly, friendly person, with an infectious smile and a good sense of humor. Like most alcoholics, she could laugh at herself and her addiction, once she had gone through withdrawal.

Her first reaction to me, she later told me, was a combination of dislike and envy. "I hate him," she said to herself, "because I'm suffering and he's a doctor. He seems to display all the advantages one imagines a doctor to have—security, comfort, money, and peace of mind—and his height makes him appear to look down on all of us."

She was on duty the next morning when I made my first thorough inspection of the infirmary. There was no sterilizer there, so I went up to my room to get one. I took it into the nurses' station, and asked Doris where to put it. She pointed to the sink board, and it was then, she later informed me, that she realized we might be on the same wave length, despite her first impression of me, because when I set the sterilizer down, my hands had a slight tremor. I didn't tell her that I wasn't quite the self-assured individual she had thought I was, but that tremor indicated to her that something was there, some insecurity or trauma. As I looked back several months later, it seemed remarkable that she had understood so much about me from something so apparently insignificant that I hadn't been aware of it myself.

Our relationship grew in the months that followed. We were both so disillusioned about love and marriage that we felt incapable of either, but we were thrown together in our work and were soon spending our time off together, as well. Once established at Riverdale, I began taking patients to weekend AA meetings around Maine, New Hampshire, and Massachusetts. Doris went along on more and more of these trips. At first we both accepted this as part of her duties, but eventually we realized that it was more personal than that. The more we saw of each other, the closer we became until, at last, we realized that we both still possessed the ability to fall in love, despite the bitterness of our previous experiences. In these early stages of our relationship, we simply accepted each other for what we were—I a drug addict and she an alcoholic—and enjoyed the present, studiously avoiding any mention of the future. Since Doris was still married and, because of her religion, apparently would never be free as long as her husband lived, we never talked about that. Yet as our romance developed, we came to think of each other as husband and wife—and, marriage or no marriage, we became so emotionally dependent upon each other that we literally held each other up.

I wish I could say that we cured each other's addictions, but it wasn't that simple. The best we could do was to give each other not only love, but understanding, sympathy, support, and the knowledge that neither of us could function well without the other. Our acceptance of each other supplemented our acceptance of ourselves, including my own eventual acceptance of my alcoholism. There were times when we seemed hopelessly immersed in the mire of despair; yet, no matter how low we sank, we were never far apart, always more concerned about each other than about ourselves.

Several months after I began working at Riverdale, a

retired army lieutenant-colonel came up from his home in
New York City to dry out after a bout with booze. While
recovering from his withdrawal, he told me that he thought
there should be more places like Riverdale for alcoholics, and
asked if I would be interested in helping him establish one.
He had a sizable trust fund, which he wanted to use for that
purpose, and offered me a partnership if I would become
chief of the medical staff. He also needed help in finding a
site and, knowing that I had lived in Maine for several years,
asked if I had any idea of where we could find one. I gave
him the names of several areas to check, and a few weeks
later he asked me to look at a place called the Carriage
House, an abandoned tourist hotel in Naples, about fifteen
miles out of Portland, on the road to Bridgton.

It had seventeen acres, with a 1,000-foot shore frontage on
a sandy beach on Brandy Pond and about 1,500 feet facing
the highway. The main house was in good repair, though it
had been empty for some time. There were twelve bedrooms
—some single, some double—a big hotel-type kitchen, a
central paneled dining room, a good-sized living room, and an
office. Besides a barn attached to the main building, the
property included several cabins with modern plumbing and
hot air heaters. Once we decided to go ahead, we began setting up legal arrangements for purchasing the property from
the woman who owned it. A Portland law office drew up the
necessary papers for incorporation, with me as president and
chief medical officer, our backer as vice-president, and Doris
as secretary-treasurer and head nurse. We were all to receive
modest salaries, since my partner would be active in the operation of the place, which we renamed Brandy Point Lodge. I
would also be given an extra stipend for each patient so that I
could meet the financial obligations set up in my divorce. I
hadn't been able to contribute anything while in the Augusta

hospital, but I had planned to send Kay money through her lawyer after starting my job at Riverdale.

As a corporation, we issued shares of voting stock, ownership of which was divided between my partner and me. We opened an account in a Portland bank and paid the owner a retainer, after which she let us move in. This was two months before papers were to be passed, but she was interested in the work and wanted to help us get started as soon as possible. While my partner traveled back and forth between Naples and New York to arrange the financial particulars and our lawyers in Portland worked on the title search and other necessary details, I spoke to the Maine alcoholic counselors about sending us patients, which they were more than willing to do. The state had no rehabilitation center for alcoholics, most of whom ended up in mental hospitals or jails. The only establishment doing anything for these people was a private hospital in Bangor. Through the State Director of Public Health, I also arranged for us to be recognized as a member organization in the hospital insurance plan to which the state subscribed.

While thrilled with the prospect of running a rehabilitation center for alcoholics, I found it hard to believe that everything was running so smoothly. As the closing date approached, I became so nervous that my back and leg pains increased, and I began wondering what to do. From long experience, I knew that this was the prelude to seeking an escape from reality, this time from something that seemed too good to be true. Although I didn't know it, Doris was watching me carefully, for she had intuitively recognized my danger signs.

One day, while she and I were shopping in Bridgton, I suddenly developed an almost panic compulsion to take narcotics, which snowballed so fast that I began to feel as though I were about to have muscle spasms. I knew that this compulsion had nothing to do with pain, because at that moment I had very little. This was my addiction, kept dormant for months, rising to the surface.

Doris peered sharply at me and said, "Are you all right, Jim?"

"Let's walk," I said.

I started walking at a fast pace, accelerated by my long stride. I didn't know where I was going, and didn't care. As I raced down one street and up the next, I was aware of Doris's increasingly heavy breathing as she practically ran to keep up with me. Not for three quarters of an hour did my compulsion taper off to a point where I could slow down. I turned and looked at Doris, now panting, her smooth brow beaded with perspiration, and I had to stifle an urge to take her in my arms right on that city sidewalk and kiss her in broad daylight. Thanks to her, the pressure was over, and with it my desire for a fix.

This was the first time I had ever resisted such a strong compulsion after such a long period of keeping clear of drugs. It had been nearly a year since the experience that had landed me in the Augusta State Hospital. If I had been alone, I would surely have taken something—probably a shot of Demerol—and that would have started me on another tragic ride down my personal road to hell.

Although I hadn't said it in so many words, I subconsciously had been thinking, as I walked, of the most important phrase in a drug addict's vocabulary: "This, too, shall pass." The trick is to make sure that it *will* pass. It may be a battle an addict can win in five or ten minutes, or it may be one that takes an hour. The more alone he feels—and one can feel very much alone in the midst of a big crowd—the harder it is to say, "This, too, shall pass," and make it stick.

Doris was as familiar with the feeling of being alone as I

was. She knew she had to keep up with me as I walked, regardless of the cost to her in energy and comfort. She knew she had to be where I could see her, not behind me but by my side. As long as she was there I knew, at the very height of my compulsion, that I wasn't alone, for she suffered with me as much as if that compulsion had been hers, too.

We were in the process of having an addition put on the main building for an infirmary when our first patients arrived. Although we didn't own the place and were still waiting for our license to operate as a hospital, state officials were already sending people to us. We could take only a limited number of patients, and, until our ownership papers were passed, our corporation completed, and our infirmary built, we accepted only those desperately in need of immediate help.

While we worked hard, we had time for the type of recreation I enjoyed most. There were plenty of chances for hunting and fishing right on our property. At Riverdale I had built a small fiberglass boat, which we had brought to Naples. I also had a couple of guns, which I took out whenever I could, usually in the company of either Doris or my partner. Often, one or both of them also went fishing in the lake with me.

The episode in Bridgton had calmed me down considerably, and for the few weeks remaining before our deal would be closed I felt good, had little pain and no compulsions. I think Doris was more perceptive than I; she could recognize my danger signs, as she had proved in Bridgton. On the other hand, I could not have recognized hers, and, to this day, I don't know if during that period she felt the same sort of need for liquor that I had felt for drugs. On the contrary, she had proven to be my stabilizing influence, and that alone made me recognize her as the stronger of the two of us.

When the lawyers summoned us to Portland to complete

the last of the steps necessary to make the deal, my partner and I went there together. There were certificates that required both our signatures, which would then have to be backed by a payment of $35,000. We went to Portland early on Friday morning. After the formalities, which took only a few minutes, I drove my partner to the airport to catch a plane for New York. There, he was to transfer the money from his trust fund to our corporation. He had a few other things to do, and told me he would be back the following Monday, first letting me know by phone when to pick him up.

I heard nothing from him on Monday, nothing on Tuesday, nothing on Wednesday. By then Doris and I were frantic, for this was not like him at all. During the time we were negotiating, he made several trips to New York, always returning just when he said he would. Neither of us knew where he could be reached. The only thing he had ever told us about his personal life was that his wife had left him because of his alcoholism and that he stayed in a hotel whenever he was in town.

Around noon on Thursday his wife called to tell me he had died suddenly in his hotel room the previous Monday. For the first few days after that we walked around like zombies, utterly crushed, unable to comprehend the enormity of what had happened. We had a few patients, but no money with which to operate—not the kind of money that such a place required. We had bills, dozens of them, that we had intended to pay when the money transfer had been completed. Now, except for a few small ones, we couldn't pay any.

I guess all that saved us from going out of our minds was the kindness of the people with whom we had been associated. The law firm sent a bill with a letter, telling me that this was only a formality; I was not to consider that I owed them anything, and they would keep the corporation intact in case I had an opportunity to start another. The woman from whom we were to purchase the property told us to forget the next payment of $2,000, and gave us permission to stay on as long as we chose without worrying about our obligations to her.

I sold my boat, trailer and guns for $150. I still had the car, but that wouldn't be for long, because I couldn't afford the next payment on it. I called the state authorities and told them that we couldn't care for any more patients. Somehow, in those few days between the time we got the bad news and the time we knew we would have to leave, we managed to get the patients we already had through the worst of their withdrawal, but we didn't have the money to do any more for them. Except for a few clothes and that $150 I had raised, Doris and I had nothing.

Depressed, discouraged, at loose ends, all we knew was that, whatever else happened, we had to stay together. At Doris's suggestion, we got into the car that wouldn't be ours much longer and started for Lawrence, Massachusetts, where her children lived. We thought we would visit them, then continue on to Boston where we would plan our next move.

We left Naples around noon, and checked into a pleasant motel in Nashua, New Hampshire, only a few miles from Lawrence. All the way down we tried cheering each other up, but didn't succeed. Yet we clung to our faith that somehow or other we'd manage, if only we could hold each other up long enough.

But I was terribly bitter, for I had been dealt a blow at precisely the time when things looked brighter than they had for years—a blow I didn't deserve. I had been in jails and hospitals, and now, with a partner who could help me remain clean of drugs, I could work my way back and help others.

God knows, I had tried hard enough—and then this had to happen. I may have learned, even gained strength from my other experiences, but I gained nothing but a shattering sense of loss from this one. If I told it to anyone who knew my history, I knew what he would think: *This is his pattern. These things that don't happen to others, happen to him. He's a loser and always will be.*

I opened the door to our motel room, and wordlessly we both walked in. It was an attractive room, modern and typical of the newer motels dotting the landscape all over America, with everything spotless—clean towels on the bathroom racks, two double beds beautifully made up, a huge dresser with shining glasses and an empty ice bucket, a widescreen television set, brochures about the motel chain and the Nashua area, and all the other trimmings. I picked up one brochure, glanced at it, then laid it down without comment, while Doris, sitting on the edge of one of the beds, watched me, her blue eyes gleaming, a slight smile on her face.

"Jim—"

"Yes?"

"We can't keep going like this. We've got to relax."

"I know."

"Let's not try to talk anything out now."

"All right."

"We'll destroy ourselves with this worry."

"I know."

"Let's forget our troubles. Let's enjoy tonight. Tomorrow will take care of itself."

"All right," I said.

Doris was looking down at the bed, drawing imaginary patterns on the spread.

"Jim?"

"Yes?"

"We've worked so hard. We've denied ourselves so much. Here we are in this beautiful motel, with a big television set—"

She looked at the glasses and the ice bucket on the dresser, then said, "Wouldn't this be a nice place to sit down, watch television, and relax with a couple of beers as if we were social drinkers?"

"I can do it," I said. "I've never had any trouble with liquor. I'm a drug addict."

"I could drink tonight," Doris said. "I don't have to drink in the morning if I drink at night."

"I certainly don't."

"If I try to drink tomorrow you can stop me."

"I know," I said. "The way you stopped me from shooting that day in Bridgton."

"We can pick each other up, Jim."

I walked over to her, bent down and kissed her.

"All right, honey."

Then I walked out, drove to the nearest liquor store, and returned with three king-sized six-packs of beer and two fifths of vodka.

XI

WE started just like social drinkers. I went to the ice machine at the end of the patio and filled up our bucket, then fixed some vodka and water for Doris and opened a bottle of beer for myself. We talked and watched television as we downed the first one, and began working on our second. We matched each other drink for drink; I drank first vodka, then beer for a chaser. I didn't expect any trouble, because I had never had any. I rationalized, as others do who won't face up to the fact that they are alcoholics: *I can handle my liquor as well as the next guy.* Until I saw the same signs I had seen in Boston and Washington, I was in my own mind a social drinker.

Inevitably, I blacked out; I did not become unconscious, but suffered a loss of memory. I can recall the next seven days only in bits—a few minutes here, a few minutes there —and Doris, who had continued to drink as heavily as I did, filled me in on much of what I had forgotten. Throughout that week I had continued to drive around aimlessly, always returning to the Nashua motel. One day I pulled up the car to a curb in Nashua and said, "I feel kind of dizzy. I don't want to get picked up for driving under the influence."

"I don't have a license," Doris said, "but I can drive."

"Okay. You can't lose what you don't have. I don't want to take a chance of losing mine."

159

So Doris drove, although I don't remember it.

Another evening, we parked across the street from a cafeteria in Nashua and went over to eat. I was pretty well bombed, and when I came out I wove my way back to the car and slid in under the wheel, while Doris, who wasn't too steady herself, got in on the other side. Just as I was about to put my foot on the starter, a man came up and said, "Sir, there's a cop standing back there watching you. I don't think you'd better start off, because you'll get arrested."

"Maybe you do show your booze a little, Jim, but how are we going to get back to the motel?" Doris said.

"I don't know. I haven't the slightest idea," I said.

"You can't drive, because that cop is watching. We need help." Then, after looking around, she added, "There's an Episcopal church—at least, that's what it says in front—right over there."

"Want to go in?" I said.

"Sure."

We thanked the man for telling us about the cop, and while I sat where I was, Doris got out of the car and headed for the church. Inside, she saw the minister, who wore a clerical collar. Not too familiar with Protestant churches, she went up and said hello, and when he asked if he could help her she said, "My husband's out in the car and he's been drinking too much. We can't get back to our motel because there's a cop watching and he'll arrest us for drunken driving. Is there any way you could help, Mr. Reverend Father?"

"Yes, I can help you," he said. "I'll drive you back to your motel."

"Wonderful," she said.

I got into the back seat, and Doris sat in front next to the minister. As we approached a liquor store, Doris, in her good alcoholic con fashion, said, "Mr. Reverend Father, would you stop at that store? You know when an alcoholic like my husband comes off booze, he has to do it gradually or he's likely to have convulsions and may die. I'm a nurse and know how to handle him, but we're out of booze."

When the minister stopped in front of the store, Doris, still conning, said, "I don't think I ought to get out, Mr. Reverend Father. If I give you the money, would you mind buying the booze for us? A fifth of vodka will be fine."

"Gladly," the minister said.

Doris gave him a five-dollar bill, and he went in and brought back the vodka, which he gave her. As he drove on, she kept telling him what a great thing he was doing for us and how much we appreciated it. At the motel he walked us to the door, and I remember thanking him profusely and hearing him say, "It's about five now. I'll drop by around nine tonight and see how you're doing."

By the time he knocked—exactly at 9:00—I was a little more "with it" but Doris was loaded. She was lying on the bed, not unconscious but unable to carry on a conversation. I recall inviting the minister to sit down, and we had a pleasant talk about the St. Elizabeth Hospital in Washington, D.C. He was leaving Nashua to become its chaplain, and I had taken some practical psychiatric work there during my medical school days. We shook hands when he left. I've often wondered what happened to him; he was a kind, understanding man.

After a week in Nashua, both Doris and I were too sick to drink any more. We lived in that horrible limbo that is one of the curses of acute alcoholism, we couldn't get drunk and we couldn't get sober. All the problems we had tried to solve had been replaced by other problems that we couldn't solve at all. We couldn't even solve the problem of getting the car back to Maine so we could turn it over to the finance company.

Still in better shape than Doris, who was very sick, I finally phoned Clem and Dotty Pooler, some AA friends of ours in Auburn, Maine, and they promised to come down to get us. I don't remember much about the trip, except that we stayed with an AA couple for a few days while we went through withdrawal. It wasn't as bad for me as for Doris, perhaps because I stopped drinking before she did, and had already been through the early stages.

Somebody got us an apartment and found me a job as a janitor in an urban renewal project, paying fifteen dollars a week. Even when Doris recovered a little, she couldn't work. She had lost her white uniform, cap, and shoes, so nursing was out for the moment. When my urban renewal job petered out, we both went to work remodeling a store out in the country for a lawyer who had bought the place. We each got a dollar an hour for what amounted to a monumental clean-up job. The place was beaten up, filthy, and loaded with dirty, useless junk. We burned some, stacked some, and scrubbed every square inch of the big old joint. It took us three or four weeks just to get it clean, then we worked another couple of weeks at painting it.

Our evenings were difficult because we had nothing to do, nothing to read, no TV to watch. We already had mutual memories, good and bad. We tried to forget the bad, talking only about the good old days at Riverdale and the great hopes we had had for Brandy Point Lodge, but we never mentioned the blowup there. Although thankful for each other, we were terribly depressed, for we seemed to be on a dead-end street, and we were both aware of where it would almost surely lead.

We found menial little jobs around town—none paid more than a dollar an hour—and went to AA meetings whenever we could. One night we took a few beers to relax, and got the first good night's sleep we had had since we arrived in Auburn. We felt guilty the next day and called Clem and Dotty, who came over to help us stay sober.

But a few days later, when we started on beer again, we couldn't stop drinking. Since we didn't eat, and were pouring everything we could find—from vodka to rotgut—into our badly abused stomachs, we both thought we were going to have D.T.'s. Somehow we got hold of Clem, and when he came over and saw how badly off we were, he said, "What do you want to do?"

"We've got to get to a hospital someplace, because we're going to die if we don't," I said.

Clem made a few calls and came back to tell us that the only place into which he could get us was the state hospital in Augusta. With great reluctance—since I still had nightmares about that sadistic doctor there—I agreed to go. The Togus Veterans Hospital was only three miles away, and by putting in for a transfer immediately, I might be accepted there because it is always easier to get into an institution from another than from the outside. We would be entering the state hospital as voluntary patients, so they couldn't hold us there indefinitely, regardless.

Doris was sent to the women's section as soon as we arrived, and I was transferred to Togus without even leaving the admissions office. Although I could have left Togus within a month, I stayed there as long as Doris was at the state hospital, which was about three months. Sick when we got there, she had a slow physical comeback, and neither of us felt that she could function normally without being in good condition. I wouldn't leave without her, because I knew that if I did I'd go right back into a disastrous addiction pattern of some sort. So, once over withdrawal, I helped the terribly short-handed Togus staff as a patient-doctor.

As soon as we were over withdrawal, Doris and I met once a week at regular card parties and dances bringing together the Togus patients and the female Augusta patients, held on alternate weeks at one institution or the other. We neither danced nor played cards, but this was the only way we could get together. You couldn't leave either place without being signed out by someone who would assume responsibility for you. We got around that by signing each other out, with Doris responsible for me when the party was at Augusta and me for her when it was at Togus. By February, 1965, with both of us in pretty good shape, we gave notice to our respective institutions of our intention to leave in about three days, with an income tax refund of $140, which Doris had just received from the government, to pay our immediate expenses. We planned to go to Boston, because that city seemed to offer the best job opportunities and because neither of us was very well-known there.

However, the afternoon we decided to go, I had a call from my lawyer in Lewiston, who told me I was to appear in superior court there the following morning on an old narcotics charge I had long since forgotten, and I decided to get out of the state fast. I told the Togus people that I had changed my mind and wanted to leave the next day, and called Doris, who did the same thing at Augusta. We agreed to meet at the bus station. I asked my lawyer to get me a continuance, which he succeeded in doing. I don't know the length of it, but at least it took off the immediate pressure, because without the continuance, there would be a warrant out for my arrest if I didn't appear in court—and I could be plucked right out of the bus to Boston.

I was afraid it would be done anyway the next morning, because I had no right to leave the state without permission. I reached the Augusta bus station ahead of Doris, bought a couple of tickets, then—assailed by the cop horrors—walked back and forth on the other side of the street. When Doris arrived, I said, "Is anybody looking for me?"

"I don't think so," she said.

"Why don't I walk around for the next five minutes and I'll get aboard the bus just before it leaves?"

"Do you want me to walk with you?"

"No," I said. "No one is after you."

Sweating with fear and seeing cops all over the place, I led the way to the back of the bus so I could watch everyone aboard. There was a stop at the New Hampshire state line, and when two men in overcoats and felt hats got in there, I figured, *This is it.* But the two paid no attention to me, and nobody ever did look for me on that narcotics charge. I was in and out of Maine several times thereafter without being picked up. Somehow or other, the whole business simply died, just as a similar charge had in Ohio. The only difference was that Ohio authorities had given me permission to leave, and Maine authorities hadn't.

We arrived in Boston late at night. Not knowing the city well enough, we couldn't find a room, and our only alternative was a hotel. We were there just a day or two when Doris received word from Clem and Dotty that they had obtained a nursing job for her in a Lewiston hospital. We debated about going back to Maine, but, with no apparent chance of either of us finding employment in Boston, we had no alternative.

Once again, we took a small, inexpensive apartment in Auburn, with Doris, working a 4:00-to-11:00 night shift, paying the expenses. I did everything I could to get a job, even applying at the state employment agency, but had no luck at all. Each day I walked Doris to the hospital, then went back to pick her up at night. We got along fairly well for five or six weeks, but my inability to contribute anything to the household income was depressing me more and more. Well aware of my feeling of uselessness, Doris kept encouraging me, telling me not to worry and assuring me that sooner or later something would break.

Something broke, all right: *me*. One night I bought two six-packs of beer on the way to the hospital to meet Doris. We drank it before going to bed, and I had my best night's sleep in weeks. I was more afraid for Doris than for me, but she woke up clear-eyed and ready to go to work when the time came. After I walked her to the hospital, I went out and bought a gallon of wine. As I drank it, I became more aware of hard pain in my legs than I had been in some time, and suddenly decided that there was only one way to stop it. I knew the pharmacist at a nearby drug store. He had begun his career in Brewer when I was in general practice and, having left before my original injury, remembered me as the well-respected doctor I had been in those days. Since he knew nothing about my subsequent history he filled my prescription for 30 cc's of Demerol, which I told him was for my ill wife. Before going to pick up Doris, I hid it under the living room couch.

Since Doris had been working nights, we had fallen into a routine of staying up for several hours after she was finished, either reading or talking, usually in the bedroom. However, I sometimes went out to the living room, and she thought nothing of it when, after she got into bed and started a book, I picked up a magazine and took it into the other room.

My legs were throbbing, my depression as deep as it had ever been, and I went right to the bathroom with a syringe and the vial of Demerol. In the manner of all junkies who had been off for a long time—I hadn't had a shot in two years—I started slowly, measuring out only 2 cc's. Instead of intravenously, I shot it intramuscularly because it takes effect more rapidly that way. However, the effect wears off more rapidly, too, and the temporary lift I received from the shot lasted only about fifteen minutes. After first listening for a turned book page so that I would know Doris was still reading, I went back and shot 4 more cc's. Again, the lift lasted only a short time. I looked at my watch, saw that it was nearly 12:30 and decided to get more Demerol before the drug store closed at 1:00. I told Doris that I was going out for cigarettes, and left. At the drug store I told the pharmacist that I had made a mistake and injected air into the vial, making the Demerol cloudy, so he let me have another 30 cc's.

Now, with plenty of Demerol, I took a shot so big that it put me "on the nod." To a junkie, being "on the nod" means that he sits numb, suspended between consciousness and unconsciousness, and, as he fixes his eyes on something, he has only good feelings—that he is traveling to far corners of the earth, that he can conquer any obstacle, overcome any future difficulty. He doesn't want to be interrupted because his thoughts are pleasant and he is relieved of fear, anxiety, and pain. I had been "on the nod" several times in the past, so there was nothing unusual about that night in Auburn.

I don't know what other junkies think when they are "on the nod," but I usually wanted to pray, because that was the only time I really felt that my prayers might be answered. Often I had thought, *As soon as I get my next shot for pain I'll be able to pray*, and this sustained me, although I inwardly feared that I was in so much trouble, mentally and physically, that I couldn't see my way out. When I prayed, I asked God to give me strength to overcome all my problems—physical and psychological, disability and inability to function.

But this time I didn't pray—I couldn't. I just sat there "on the nod," vaguely aware that Doris was reading in the next room and that I was doing something that, even though temporarily, relieved me of pain, depression, and pressure. Actually, I was hallucinating. Imagining that someone was asking me questions (I could hear whoever it was), I answered aloud. Then, as the effects of the most recent shot wore off, I returned to the reality and the realization that Doris might have heard me talking to myself. I listened carefully for a book page to turn, and when it did, I went back to the bathroom and shot another load. This went on until the last of the Demerol was gone.

Now the pleasant hallucinating was over, to be replaced by fear—not of withdrawal, but fear that if I were able to get more narcotics I would keep right on shooting, and wouldn't stop until I was locked up or dead. I knew then that my only chance was to tell Doris what I had done. She was still reading when I walked into the bedroom and said, "Honey, did you hear me talking in the next room?"

"No," she said. Then, "Did you drink a lot today?"

"No."

"You look as if you did."

"No," I said again. "I didn't drink much. I have to tell you what I did. I ordered two vials of 30 cc's of Demerol. I told the pharmacist, who knew me before I got hurt in Brewer, that they were for you. I shot them all tonight, and now I'm scared. I'm afraid I won't stop, and I want to. I haven't ordered any narcotics for a couple of years, and this time I ordered them in your name. If I get picked up I'll tell them I gave you a shot and threw the rest away because, being a junkie, I didn't want it around."

I sank down on the bed beside her, put my head in my hands and wept inside, although no tears came. Doris put her arms around me, lifted my head, cradled it in her lap and whispered, "Jim, you're all right. You hear me? You're all right. You *can* stop."

"I'm going to end up in withdrawal or kill myself."

"And what do you think will become of me?"

"Honey, I can't stop."

"You *will* stop. You will—you will—"

"I have to," I said.

And I did. Since that night in Auburn in the winter of 1965, I have never taken a shot or a pill except under medical supervision when I was sick or in unbearable pain. In the early years after that, I sometimes had urges out of which Doris either talked or walked me, but I never slipped into a drug pattern again. Even today, I sometimes feel a little uneasy, but never beyond either my own or Doris's control.

But I couldn't stop drinking. In the days immediately following the Demerol episode, I drank myself into a stupor. One night Doris came home from work, found me unconscious on the floor, and could detect no respiration and only a very weak pulse, so she called an ambulance. I was so far out of it—the Demerol effects had still not worn off completely—that the hospital called the police, who came to the emergency ward to which I had been taken. It took less than an hour to bring me around, and I went right from the ward to the police station. I remember the officers asking if I would give them permission to record their interrogation of me, and my answering, "Yes." That's the only recollection I have of the interrogation that night.

I woke up the next morning hearing someone yell, "Hey, junkie doctor, wake up. You're on the air."

I looked around and saw that I was alone in a jail cell about four by eight feet. I lay there trying to remember what happened, but couldn't. Every so often, someone yelled, "Hey, junkie doctor." Then the same voice called, "Listen, junkie doc, you're on again. You hear me? Listen, you like this?"

This time I heard a brief news report, which, in effect,

said, "Late last night, James C. DeWitt, M.D., was arrested for writing false narcotics prescriptions." That was all, but it was enough. Everyone in Auburn and Lewiston, which are twin cities, now knew what I was and who I was.

I continued to lie on the jail cot, torn apart inside, trying to piece things together. I was still trying, when an officer came to tell me that I was being held on narcotics charges, my bail set at $2,000, and that my case was coming up in a few minutes. Not long after that, two other officers came to get me. As they escorted me along a steel passageway with cells on both sides, the kids kept yelling, "Hey, junkie doctor, what are you going to get? Are you guilty? You know you're guilty, junkie doctor. They'll throw the book at you."

I waited half an hour before my case came up, while the judge rapidly disposed of one small case after another, mostly traffic charges. When my turn came, he asked if I had a lawyer or could afford one, and after I said, "No," he told me that the court would appoint one. He directed an officer to take me out to the corridor, where I would be met by the lawyer. He turned out to be a kid who must have been fresh out of law school. His briefcase was shiny, and he was filled with the self-importance of the young. I had known dozens of doctors like him; in fact, I had been one myself, I guess. The newest, least experienced professional men always think they know the most. Sometimes it takes you years to discover how little you know, how much you still have to learn.

It happened that I knew more about the law than he. After he introduced himself, he said, "I hear you're charged with a narcotics violation."

"That's right," I said.

He reached into his briefcase, pulled out a new book of Maine laws and punishments, and said, "Well, let's see what that calls for." He checked the index, leafed through the book, found what he was looking for, and said, "That's a $500 fine and a minimum of one year in prison for a first offense. Did you do it?"

"You're my lawyer, aren't you?" I said.

"Yes."

"Are you defending me?"

"Yes. We'll go back in the courtroom and plead guilty."

"What?"

"That's the way the law should be. If you're guilty of a crime and know you're guilty, you should plead guilty."

"I can't do that. You just told me what the punishment is."

"The laws should be observed as they are written."

"Young man," I said, "the judge appointed you as my attorney. I appreciate your help, but when we go back into that courtroom and my name is called, you just sit there by the bar and let me do the talking."

Back in the courtroom, I stepped up to the box, and when the judge asked me my plea, I said, "Not guilty, your honor."

I was then escorted back to my cell. I hadn't been there five minutes when two plainclothesmen came in, one identifying himself as a state narcotics agent and the other as a city detective-lieutenant.

"Doc," the agent said, "I'm sure you can raise bail to get out, but since we locked you up I checked statewide and found these were the first prescriptions you had written in over two years. A junkie who has been off that long can keep off indefinitely. If we let you go now you might start right in again. But if you stay here for ten days, you'll be clean and maybe stay that way if we let you out then."

"Thanks," I said. "That's the first intelligent approach to addiction I've ever heard expressed by a police officer. I'll stay."

I didn't ask about the old charge that was supposed to be hanging over my head. He must have known about it, but didn't mention it. We shook hands all around, and they left. An hour later, Doris came to see me, and said she was leaving her job and going to her sister's house in Massachusetts while I served my time. When it was up, she would come back to get me.

There's never anything good about being in jail. There are only degrees of badness. The ten days I spent in the jail were not bad. I've done much worse time, for much longer, in mental institutions.

XII

WHEN I phoned Doris in Massachusetts as soon as I was released from jail, I could tell she had been drinking, but it didn't bother me. I had learned the type of understanding that always meant so much to both of us. We recognized the nature of each other's illnesses, and when one or the other slipped we saw it in the same light as a mother sees a stomach ache, for example, in a child. I knew that when Doris arrived in Auburn on the 11:30 bus that night she would need help, and I was prepared to help her.

I spent a good part of the day raising $150 by cashing in my last life insurance policy. Then, since we had given up the apartment, I checked into a cheap hotel because I would have to appear in court the following morning. At the bus station, Doris and I greeted each other with hugs, kisses, and tears of happiness. Except for a slight personality change, she gave no sign that she had been drinking, and she told me in the hotel room that she knew she could stop if I helped her.

Although the judge gave me a continuance of several months at the hearing the next morning, I was uneasy, because there had been some local publicity about my release from jail. I thought that everyone who saw me recognized the junkie doctor, and I wanted to get out of town quickly. Much of this was my imagination running wild, as it always

173

did when I got into trouble with the law, but it felt very real to me. I picked up Doris and checked out of the hotel, and the two of us took a bus to Portland. On the way, we discussed our troubles, which is always dangerous for alcoholics. Among other things, I was terrified of further failure. My inability to get a job in Auburn meant to me that I wouldn't be able to do any better in Portland. After a while I got on a variety of subjects—my lost children, my lost self-respect, the indictments (which, as far as I knew then, were still hanging over my head), my loss of hope, and my need for escape. Doris, who couldn't stop drinking herself, kept soothing me, telling me that when we reached Portland I would find refuge from my fears, which magnified as I counted up my troubles. The first thing we did in Portland was to rent a room; the second, to buy a couple of fifths of vodka; the third, to start drinking them.

Doris sobered up when we ran out of money. With me going half crazy for want of any relief, she found an old AA friend in town whom I had treated at Riverdale. He and his wife came right over to be with me while Doris went out and found a nursing job in a Portland hospital. I guess we were all afraid that I might slip back into a drug pattern, but a drink would have served the same purpose. Although I was not yet thoroughly aware of it, my alcoholism had replaced my addiction.

Our friends called in an alcoholic counselor, who told me that if I wanted to go somewhere to get off booze he would pay for a week in an alcoholic rehabilitation center for me. I agreed, Doris found someone to take her in, and the counselor drove me to a home in New Hampshire called Beech Hill Farm. The worst part of the whole experience was the trip up there. I wasn't drunk, but I was so sick that I thought I would have a convulsion.

Once there, however, I had no problem. After being pulled through six days of withdrawal with medication, I felt well enough to work, and was given a job as an attendant for sick entering alcoholics. I put in regular eight-hour shifts, and kept at it for three weeks at a modest salary. Both Doris and I were trying to save enough to get another start together and perhaps begin a new life. This was always our only hope. Somewhere, somehow, someday, we would find a way to get off this aimless, mindless alcoholic merry-go-round. Even when we were both on it, we knew we had to stay together if we were ever to find the peace of mind so necessary for success. Singly, we would fall apart and never pick up the pieces. Together, we had a chance.

Full of optimistic new resolutions, we met in Gardner, Massachusetts, which is fairly near Beech Hill Farm and on a bus route from Portland. Happy as we were to be together, we realized, as we tried to figure out where to go and what to do next, that there was a rough road ahead. The trouble was, we were both shooting higher in our minds than we could possibly reach at that point. We thought we had been accepting jobs too menial, and looking to futures too indefinite. This time, we decided, we'd work out a plan that would offer us a better life than we had ever enjoyed together, perhaps I might even build up to a return to medical practice. I would get my children, Doris would get hers (she had two) and everything would work out well. As a matter of fact, we did have one thing going for us. Despite her husband's Catholicism, Doris had heard, he planned to sue for divorce. If he did, she wouldn't contest it, and we would then be able to get married.

We checked into a hotel room in Gardner, spent the early afternoon at a movie, then purchased hamburgers and coffee and ate in the room. It was about 3:00, neither lunch nor supper time. Again, we spoke about the future, although not in such rosy terms. When we touched on the subject of our children, whom we both missed desperately, the world began looking dark again. One thing led to another, until we could see nothing but insoluble problems. We magnified the small ones and worried about the big ones, becoming more and more tense, frustrated, and depressed. Inevitably, we reached the point that all alcoholics reach: *If we can just relax our minds now with a little drink or two, we'll be able to think more clearly. We'll be able to quit, all right. We won't get drunk or anything. We can keep things under control. And afterwards we can work things out together.*

We were too broke to buy vodka, so I went out and picked up a gallon of wine. Neither of us liked wine, but it was the cheapest booze with the most alcohol for the price. I poured us each a glassful, and we drank it the only way we could—first swallowing a few times, then taking a deep breath, then drinking, then holding our breath long enough to keep it down. We never ate, slept only in snatches, lost track of time, place, everything—just kept on drinking. Somehow, I guess, I must have gotten more wine. We didn't want it, hated the taste, knew we were getting into trouble, didn't know how to get out of it, didn't know where to go, didn't know how to stop drinking.

Three foggy days went by that way before a guy I had known at Beech Hill came into the room and said, "Come on, doc. I'm getting you out of here. This is my town and I know everyone here. The manager called and said the two of you haven't been out of the room in a couple of days."

He drove us to a nursing home in New Hampshire where Doris had once worked and knew the owners were always looking for help. She got a job as a combination nurse and cook, on call twenty-four hours a day but actually just working twelve. I tried half-heartedly to get a job, but I couldn't shake my depression, and started drinking again. Finally, with all hope gone, I told Doris that I wasn't going to stop, and that the only way I ever could was to go into a hospital somewhere. Without money to go to a private hospital, we called the Concord State Hospital and they agreed to take me as a voluntary patient for ten days. A friend of Doris's who had a car agreed to drive me there. Doris picked up some vodka and mix and gave me the two bottles to drink, because that was the only way I could have endured the trip, which was about 40 miles. The girls sat together in front, while I killed the whole bottle and all the mix in the back. By the time we arrived at the hospital, I was so loaded that I couldn't sign my name as a voluntary patient. The only alternative was for the doctor to commit me, which he did.

When I woke up the next morning, two doctors were standing beside my bed in a locked ward. It took me a few minutes to realize where I was and how I got there; then I said, "I'll sign that paper now."

"What paper?" one of the doctors asked.

"For my admission as a voluntary patient so I can get out in ten days."

"You're not a voluntary patient."

My heart stopped, as I thought of those six months in Augusta, and my throat was so constricted that it took a couple of moments before I could say, "What do you mean?"

"You couldn't sign the paper last night, so you had to be committed by the doctor on duty."

My God, here I am at the mercy of somebody else again, I thought. *I wonder how long they'll make me stay. If I get another guy like that one in Maine, I'm a dead pigeon.*

But I didn't get another doctor like the one in Maine; in fact, the people in Concord were very good to me and seemed to understand that I was not a criminal but a sick man. Besides, Doris knew I was there, and on my second weekend she came to see me. I remember the warmth I felt as I heard the click of her heels and saw the big smile on her face as she approached me. I stood up and kissed her, and we started to talk about my getting out.

After about half an hour, I walked over to the water fountain to get a drink and passed an elderly patient with whom I had become friendly.

"Doc," he said loudly enough for Doris to hear, "your daughter sure is beautiful."

I didn't know whether to laugh or cry, so I compromised by thanking him without bothering to explain.

The doctors told Doris that they thought I should stay quite a while, because my blood tests showed I was in such bad shape that if I didn't get off the drug and booze pattern soon I wouldn't live six months. However, after she told them I was off drugs, they decided to give me a hearing at a staff meeting the next day. As always, I rehearsed the questions and answers, and how I would act. I would stride into the room with confidence, smile, look relaxed, and assure everyone that I was all right and would remain that way.

But at the meeting the staff chairman did most of the talking. He told me that I was a hopeless addict and alcoholic, and that the staff had two choices—either to keep me for a period of years, during which I would at least stay alive because I couldn't abuse myself, or to let me out at the end of 21 days, the minimum stay for a patient in a New Hampshire state hospital. After some open discussion, while I held my breath, the doctors finally decided to let me out when the 21 days were up, which would be in less than a week. Then they returned me to the ward.

Doris took a bus to Concord the day I was released, and

the two of us checked into a tenth-rate hotel that didn't even have locks on the doors. All we had between us was the $45 Doris had earned in the nursing home. Although happy to be together again, we felt hopeless, lost, and unwanted. It was one of the few times I can recall when a reunion between us didn't result in new plans, new resolutions, new optimism. Depressed as we were, we started drinking as soon as we could buy a gallon of wine, and we didn't stop until we went broke two days later.

We decided we had to get to Maine. Don't ask me why, for we had suffered as much trouble and as many setbacks there as anywhere else. But alcoholics think that way. They can't really make it anywhere as long as they keep on drinking, but wherever they are, the grass always looks greener somewhere else to them. I guess in our wine-inspired fog we figured that Clem and Dotty might help us, although we truly didn't know what they could do. All we knew was that we weren't going anywhere in New Hampshire, and Maine seemed as good a place as any.

Both of us were sick, but we had no money to buy any booze in order to get well for a few hours before getting sick again, and we couldn't afford transportation. So, with Doris carrying my small suitcase and me taking her larger one, we walked out of town. I guess we went two or three miles before starting to hitchhike, but the only ride we could finally get was with a guy who had to let us off in the middle of nowhere because he was leaving the main road.

It started raining just as evening fell, and we went into the woods to seek shelter and keep out of the way of state cops who, we were afraid, might pick us up for vagrancy. I found a place where I could spread out a couple of old shirts from my suitcase, pulled some branches off low-hanging trees for a little protection from the rain, took off my jacket to use as a blanket, and lay down with Doris at my side. I guess we must have slept a bit, but most of the night we just talked about ourselves; Doris crying and shivering as I held her in my arms. We reviewed our lives, and all we could find in the past was heartbreak, frustration, and failure. I remember thinking, over and over, *There must be some way we can stop drinking booze.* We had tried everything, and nothing worked. Before we knew each other I had tried alone to stay off drugs and she had tried alone to stop drinking. After we knew each other we had tried together to quit drinking. Maybe I was off drugs and maybe I wasn't, but I was certainly on booze and so was Doris. Once, as she dozed in my arms, I lay back thinking, *Why can't I lie on a rug in a nice, warm house with Doris beside me? Why do we have to lie here, cold and wet, miserable and sick?*

After a while it stopped raining, but that didn't make us any more comfortable. At dawn, we struggled to our feet, I holding up Doris because she felt so weak. We hadn't eaten in nearly two days or had a drink in nearly 24 hours. When we had put the damp shirts back in my suitcase we went to the edge of the road to hitchhike, but it was early Sunday morning and no cars came for a long time.

"I'm sick, Jim," Doris said when we reached the road. "I think I'm going to pass out or have a convulsion."

"Sit on the suitcase and put your head down."

I rubbed her neck gently, waiting for something to come along, but there wasn't a car in sight. We started walking when Doris said she felt a little better. After we had gone about a mile, an elderly man came along in a pickup truck that looked older than he did. When he stopped and asked where we were going, I said, "Waterville, Maine," because Clem and Dotty had gone there to live.

"Well," he said, "I'm just heading for the next village to go to Mass. You might as well come along. You'll have a better chance of getting a ride out of there."

Opposite the church where he was going was a pretty little village green, and I told Doris to sit on a bench there and wait for me. I stood for a minute watching the people, all dressed up, happy and smiling as they went in to Mass, and I thought, *Wouldn't it be wonderful if two of those people were Doris and I? If we could be clean inside and out, and thank God for our blessings?*

Noticing a state police car moving slowly by, I crossed over to the church, went up the stairs and said to the priest greeting people, "May I talk to you a minute?"

"I've got to go in and say Mass now," he said. "But I'll be glad to talk to you when it's over."

I thanked him and went down the steps and headed for a little grocery store, the only place in town aside from the churches, that seemed to be open. There was a woman alone to wait on customers, but there weren't any when I walked in.

"Can I help you?" she asked.

"Not right away," I said. "I'm just looking around."

I spotted a six-pack of beer in back of the store, and, when a man came in for cigarettes, I took two cans out of it and slipped them under my shirt. Then, while the saleswoman was ringing up the man's money on the cash register, I turned the six-pack around so that the gaps wouldn't show. As I eased toward the door she asked if I had found anything I wanted, and I said, "No."

When I got out of the store, I was shaking from booze withdrawal, fear, and the guilt of stealing. Except for those drugs at the hospital long before, I had never in my life taken anything that didn't belong to me. I had always tried to maintain my honesty in thought and action, but now I thought, *I'm too sick to be honest.* Doris saw me coming, and rose from the bench to meet me. When I told her about the beer, we went behind the store. There, after opening them with the can opener in my pocket, we each took one can, but that didn't help much. One can of beer won't cure booze-sickness for more than a few minutes.

Back on the village green, I sat with Doris, waiting for Mass to end so I could speak with the priest. As it turned out, I never did get a chance to do so, because the police cruiser pulled up on the street in front of us and the officer in it called out, "Hey, buddy, come here."

When I got there, he said, "What are you doing?"

"Just sitting and resting a minute."

"Where are you going?"

"Maine."

"What for?"

"I've got a job there," I said.

The officer was young and rugged, neither tough nor challenging, but he kept asking one question after another.

"Got any identification?"

I handed him my beaten-up old wallet, and the first thing he pulled out was my medical card. He raised his eyebrows in surprise and said, "Are you really a doctor?"

"That's right."

"Who's the lady?"

"My wife."

"How come you're on the bum?"

"We had a little bad luck," I said.

"Where did you come from?"

"Concord. I just got out of the state hospital there."

"Go join your wife on the bench while I do some checking," he said.

I went back and sat down beside Doris. She thought we

should start walking out of town, but I told her we couldn't leave until the cop had checked us out. The car was close enough for us to hear the other end of the conversation on the loudspeaker, and the last thing I heard before the cop came back to the bench was, "Those two people you have are not wanted in the state. They're probably going where they said, because the rest of their story is true."

The cop then asked us if we had any money, and we told him we were broke. Then he said, "Do you know you could be picked up for vagrancy?"

"I know," I said.

"You shouldn't hitchhike from here," he said. "One of the local cops will grab you. Look—I've only been on the police force a few months, so I've got to check with my sergeant. If it's okay, I'll drive you to the Maine border."

"How far is it?"

"Hundred miles," he said.

Just outside of town he pulled up in front of a diner and went inside for several minutes. He came out with two white sacks, one with hamburgers and coffee, the other with two packs of cigarettes, and when he gave them to me I split them up with Doris. When I tried to tell him how much we appreciated it, he said, "There have been times when I needed help and there'll be more times, so forget it."

It took about two and a half hours to get to the border. Before leaving us off, the cop wrote down his name, call number, and the barracks to which he was attached, and told us to call him if the Maine State Police picked us up. Then, waving away my thanks, he turned around and started back.

We looked so bad that we had a tough time getting rides towards Waterville, and we were becoming more and more ill from withdrawal pains. When we were dropped off near a country store in the late afternoon, I asked Doris, "Have you anything at all for which we can get some money? We both need something to pull us out of this."

After looking through her things, she found 60¢ worth of postage stamps. I went into the store and asked the man if he'd give us a 45¢ quart of beer for them.

"I would, but you can't sell beer in Maine on Sundays," he said.

"My wife and I are going to have convulsions and maybe die if we don't get something."

The man looked around, then took the stamps and gave me the beer.

"I wouldn't ordinarily do this, but I can tell you're sick just by looking at you," he said. "Hide the beer when you go out because I'll get into trouble if I get caught."

Doris and I went into the woods, where I opened the bottle by prying the cap loose on a sharp rock. We each drank from it, taking small swallows to make it last longer, and it made us feel a little better. Then we started hitch-hiking again and made Waterville by about 10:00 that night. I didn't want to call Clem and Dotty because we both looked so awful, but I would have if I hadn't bumped into a guy we both knew from AA. When we told him our story, he said that he had an extra key to AA headquarters.

"It's empty on Sundays," he said, "so you can stay there."

We did that, and had a pretty good night's sleep. I saw Clem the next day; he found us a room, and the day after that got me a job as a janitor for two old adjoining houses, for which they gave me sixteen dollars a week and a room for the two of us. Although we were both sick from withdrawal, we managed to clean the place up a little, and a week later Doris felt well enough to take a nursing job.

We hadn't exactly hit the jackpot, but, for the moment, at least, we were back in business.

XIII

WE stayed in Waterville and out of trouble for about four months. While we were there I received a notice from the Maine authorities that due to my narcotics record, they had cause to revoke my license to practice. I was to appear at a special hearing in Augusta on a certain date, and failure to do so would be considered an admission of guilt. I didn't go, because it wouldn't have done any good. In due course, I received notification that my state license had been taken away, and with it my federal license to dispense narcotics. This meant that I couldn't practice or write prescriptions anywhere in the United States—a rather minor blow, since I hadn't been doing either for over a year anyway. I did get one good break—the narcotics charge that had landed me in the Lewiston jail was lifted for lack of evidence of my continued drug use (I was too busy drinking).

There was nothing wrong with Waterville, but nothing particularly good about it either. We had no feeling of permanence there. Doris was doing pretty well, but I couldn't get more than an odd job here and there. We both agreed to try Boston again, and when we had saved enough money for bus fare and a few days' expenses on arrival, we left for that city. On the way, we started discussing all our problems—with results that were predictably disastrous. As soon as we arrived in town, we checked into a cheap hotel and started drinking.

The next three or four days are almost a total blank in my memory, with only bits of recollection scattered like patches of sky in a fog. I remember going back for more booze and returning to the room, starting with vodka and eventually getting down to wine. And Doris told me later that at some point we were in the bus terminal, both so drunk that a cop approached us. She said that, on checking her papers, he found she was registered as a nurse in Maine and said something about making arrangements for her to take a bus back there. I remember, then, taking off while he was talking to her, probably, I suppose, because I was scared. When sober and off drugs I worked with the police; when drunk or on drugs, I was afraid of them.

I remember, too, waking up the following morning in a shabby room with no door to the corridor. I got up, feeling very sick, with about 40¢ in my pocket, wondering where I was and where Doris could be. I combed my hair and went to the nearest police station, where I asked if Doris had been picked up the night before for drunkenness. While I sat on a bench and worried, the desk sergeant, after making some phone calls, told me that Doris had been, and still was, in the women's detention section of the courthouse jail. I left without asking any more questions, because I was afraid of being questioned myself. Out on the street a cop told me where the courthouse was. When I found it and asked for the women's detention section, I was told that there wasn't any there, that I must have meant the courthouse in Boston.

"I thought I was in Boston," I said.

"No," the officer at the information counter said, "this is South Boston." Then, pointing from the window to a high building that looked a long distance away, he said, "That's the one you mean."

Once again I left without asking questions. So sick that I

thought I might go into a convulsion, I started walking in the general direction of the downtown courthouse, but couldn't make it. I had just about enough money for subway fare, and finally found the place. There, the matron told me that Doris was in a cell but would soon be called into court, and that if I vouched for her she would undoubtedly be released. She let me talk to Doris for a few minutes, and later on, in court, the judge dismissed her case.

We were sick, miserable, and broke, but somehow found our way back to the original hotel to pick up our luggage. The desk clerk was a friendly guy who not only let us have our things, but told us we could use his phone to call AA. When we asked the operator for the number, she gave us the Center for Alcoholics and Homeless Persons, a research project that existed downtown then, but later moved to the South End, Boston's Skid Row. Some of that area still is the same, although several sections have been improved by urban renewal projects.

The people at the Center told us to wait for a man to pick us up, since it was a bitter-cold day. He checked us into the Center, then found us a room, took us there, and gave us two dollars for food. Both Doris and I were at a complete loss. Neither of us had ever seen anything like the South End, with its smelly bars, its shabbily dressed people both black and white, and its slobbering drunks, some unconscious on doorsteps or in gutters, others sick and drooling, and a few swaying on their feet as they tried to bum enough change for wine. In pretty horrible shape ourselves, we agreed to stop drinking even if it killed us (I guess it pretty nearly did, for we were both suffering intense withdrawal pains), and Doris remembered an AA couple who had gone to see her in jail and left her a number to call. They took us to an AA meeting that night, then back to the Center, where we were given a card that entitled us to apply for relief. This, too, was a new situation for me. It was my first lesson on how to survive on Skid Row.

At the relief office, where we went the next morning, a social worker assigned to us asked about my education and personal history, and why I wasn't practicing medicine.

"I can't," I said. "I lost my license."

"But a man of your background should be able to get a job," he said.

"A man of my background has a tougher time getting a job than a fourth-grade dropout. The minute people find out I'm an M.D., all they have to do is look at me and they know something's wrong. I'm a junkie and an alcoholic, and I can't do heavy work on account of my back."

I told him about my physical problems and asked if he knew where I could get a job. He didn't, but he gave us a relief check that paid for our room, with a little left over for food. Doris's friend had given her a schedule of AA meetings, and we went to one somewhere in the city—sometimes we walked five or six miles—each night for nineteen nights in a row. We took no part in these meetings, but merely listened to the speakers, got in line for doughnuts and coffee, went off into corners to eat, then walked back to the room.

Beaten down, we didn't know which way to turn. We tried a Catholic church, going daily to the Cathedral of the Holy Cross in the South End to pray. I couldn't get a job, but finally found a place where I could sign my name on a board for dishwashing jobs if any came up. That way, I managed to work about once every four or five days, collecting a dollar and a quarter an hour, which helped us eat a little more than we could buy with what was left over from the relief checks after we had paid our room rent.

Besides being a haven for drunks, the South End was dangerous after dark, so when we walked home from AA meetings we reversed the normal courtesy procedure, with Doris on the outside so I would be nearer to the doorways. Although I couldn't fight my way out of a paper bag because of my back, I guess my size scared people off, so nobody tried to attack us.

After about three weeks of this aimless existence, with everything lost, nothing but a dim light bulb and a dirty bed in our dingy room, and everyone around us reflecting our own despair, we finally decided that we had to get some wine and relax for just one night. That started us on another alcoholic cycle. We drank to pass out so that we wouldn't have to face life. We had blackouts and kept getting separated, sometimes unable to find each other for three or four days. How we managed I'll never know, because the blackouts almost completely blocked our memories. We just found each other by instinct, I guess, meeting in the room, stumbling into each other's arms, sick to death of life yet somehow realizing that we couldn't live without each other.

During a lucid period when we were together, I remembered having heard that there was an alcoholic clinic at the Massachusetts General Hospital; we went down there, looking for someone who had the nonexistent magic formula to get us out of this pattern. After we waited a couple of hours, a doctor came in. I recognized his name as that of an authority on alcoholism, and thought surely he could help us. But when he heard my history of drugs and booze, he glared at me in disgust and said, "It's obvious that you're addicted to both, whichever happens to be most handy." I didn't need him to tell me this. I needed someone who could stop me from drinking because I couldn't stop myself. Before I had the words out, he turned and walked away without even looking at Doris, who was sicker than I (she always was when we were both drinking).

I thought, *The hell with this great alcoholic specialist.*

*Maybe there's a psychiatrist somewhere with a heart to go
with his brain.* There was, a young fellow in the acute psychiatric emergency ward. I showed him our relief cards and
asked if there were some way that Doris could be admitted to
the hospital. He said there were only a few beds for alcoholics, but he'd try to get her one. When he did, I said,
"Goodbye," to her, told her I'd see her the next day, and
walked back to the South End.

I felt so depressed, so scared and helpless in the room, that
I knew I couldn't make it through the night alone. I asked
the proprietress to lend me a dollar, which I promised to pay
back when I got my welfare check, and she did. I used it to
buy a quart of wine. After I drank it, I got a full night's sleep,
and woke up so sick that I couldn't make it to the hospital to
see Doris. This went on for the next three or four days, with
the woman giving me a dollar each day and me buying a
quart of wine that made me too sick to get to the hospital. I
was worried about Doris. I knew that she expected me and I
was afraid that she might not understand why I didn't show
up.

Finally, I went to the Center for Alcoholics, told some
staff members that my wife was in the Massachusetts General
Hospital, and asked if they could get me in there. They said
that they couldn't do that, but that if I would sign a paper
promising to stay voluntarily for fifteen days, they could get
me into the Massachusetts Correctional Institution at Bridgewater, which had a special unit for alcoholics. The place also
handled mental cases, and later won national notoriety
through a harrowing movie called *Titicut Follies*, purporting
to show the callousness of its treatment of mental patients. I
always thought that this gave Bridgewater a bum rap, because, as bad as things were there, they were no worse than in
any other state mental hospital I have ever seen or heard of.
At any rate, I signed the paper, the Center people called

Doris to tell her where I was going and when I'd be out, and, after an hour or so, five of us—all swollen-faced and sick from living too long on nothing but alcohol—were taken to Bridgewater in a station wagon.

All I knew about that place was what alcoholic patients of mine had told me in New Hampshire, that it was a typical drying-out joint, no different from any other. When we arrived, we were herded into a big basement room, with a couple of guards sitting on a platform, alternately looking at papers in their hands and yelling instructions. We took off our vomit-saturated clothes and got under showers, with the guards bellowing things such as, "Scrub their heads! Turn the lights off! Put their shoes in the bucket!" They gave all kinds of orders, and I didn't know what to do. I was shaking and hoping it would be over quickly, so I could lie on a bed and suffer in silence.

After the shower, I was given patched, torn prison clothes and told to find a pair of shoes from a big, scrambled pile. The pair I found weren't mates, but they did fit. In the meantime, a guard was calling names, and when he came to mine he asked for my address. I just said, "South End," because I couldn't remember any more. At last we were led across a cement courtyard and up some steps on the other side into an old building and a huge room with about 25 ancient, high, hospital-type iron beds with sagging mattresses and dirty sheets that obviously hadn't been changed since they were last slept on. I asked which bed was mine, and another inmate told me to grab an empty one anywhere. Just as I sat down, there was an announcement over the public address system: "All VA's who came in today, report to the desk." I asked a guy if there was a special place for veterans, and when he looked blankly at me I said, "Isn't that what a VA is?"

"No," he said. "VA means voluntary admission."

I struggled back to my feet, asked how to get to the desk, and was told to go out to the corridor and down one flight. I saw someone smoking in the corridor and asked if I could bum a cigarette. He just looked at me and muttered, "Are you a nut?" When I asked someone else for his butt, the person took three or four quick drags and handed me one so short that a single drag burned my lips. Then, trembling and praying that a nurse would come around with some kind of medication, I went back to my bed and lay down without getting to the desk.

Somebody said it was chow time, and when I saw guys carrying trays into the ward, I went up to get some food. I didn't know if I could eat or not. I hadn't for about three days, and, since I had been vomiting blood, I doubted that I could keep anything down. Even under the best of conditions, it would have been a pretty horrible meal—a shrunken hot dog, a tepid potato, a scoop of cold sauerkraut, a spoonful of peaches and a cup of weak, lukewarm tea. All I could hold down was half a peach, and that gave me such cramps that I had to go to the john, where I lost it.

When I asked a very thin young man in the next bed, about four feet away, if you were kept in this place the whole fifteen days, he said, "No, this is the hospital. How long you stay depends upon which doctor is on duty. Some keep you 24 hours, some 48. After that, you'll be sent somewhere else and assigned to a work detail."

"Is this your first time here?"

"Hell, no. It's about my thirty-fifth."

"Ever been sentenced?" I asked.

"No. I always come on my own."

"When you're here once, how can you ever come back voluntarily?"

He shrugged and said, "Where else can you go to dry out?"

As time dragged on, I thought I'd go out of my mind from withdrawal pains. I asked the thin guy next to me if they gave you any medication and he said, "A goofer [sleeping capsule] at bedtime." Later, a nurse accompanied by a guard came around with capsules and a cup of some liquid. I took a capsule, drank the liquid, and went to the john, the only place where there was any water. I drank about three more cupfuls, then breathed with my mouth open to make sure I wouldn't vomit and lose the capsule. It relaxed me a bit, but I was shaking too much to sleep more than a couple of hours.

Breakfast the next morning consisted of cold cereal and milk, coffee so weak that you couldn't taste anything but a little sugar in the bottom of the cup, and a piece of dry toast, all of which I managed to eat and keep down. Just as I lay back on the cot, the VA's were summoned to the desk over the PA system. That time I made it, although I had an odd experience on the way, when a guard yelled, "What the hell's wrong with you?"

"Nothing," I said.

"What are you doing on that line then?"

I looked down and saw that I was walking on a white line drawn along the floor. Prisoners—and I was one, not a patient—weren't supposed to touch or cross the line.

Downstairs, I was mugged and fingerprinted, then told to go back to the ward. Thankful for the chance to lie down, I flopped down on the bed, but had to struggle up when the VA's were called to the desk again. That time it was for a chest X ray. I was hardly back in bed when we were called down a third time, for physicals. The doctor who examined me was an elderly man who looked at my record and asked if I were really an M.D.

"That's right."

"Then what the hell are you doing here?"

"I'm a drunk."

"You're a disgrace. Were you in the service?"

"Yes," I said. "In the Navy during World War II. I was a landing craft officer."

"I'm going to have all your Navy rights taken away from you."

"Go ahead. I don't have anything to do with the Navy anymore."

"I don't care," he said, "I'll have them taken away, regardless."

As I was beginning to wonder whether he was a doctor or a mental patient, he told me to look at an anatomical drawing of a man on the wall. He started going over it, organ by organ, telling me which ones were destroyed by alcohol. I tolerated it as long as I could, then finally said, "I probably know more about that than you do, but it doesn't stop me from drinking."

"We'll take away all your Navy rights," he said. "Maybe that will stop you."

End of physical.

Back in the ward I had about an hour of rest, when another call came. I was suffering severe back and leg pains, which were always most acute when I was coming off booze or drugs. At the desk, we were taken to another building and assigned work details, to begin the next morning. My job was in the laundry, shaking out wet clothes and bed linens so they could be put on the mangles for ironing. I did that all day for the next thirteen days of my self-imposed sentence.

We were permitted to write one letter. I sent mine to Doris, addressing it to the Massachusetts General Hospital and telling her to meet me at our room in the South End. Just before I left Bridgewater, I had a letter from her, saying she would try to get out at the same time I did. Upon my release, I got a ride into town with John Metevier, the chief social worker at Bridgewater. A fine, sensitive, patient man, he seemed instinctively to understand the problems of addiction, and in the months that followed, during which I returned to Bridgewater four more times on voluntary admissions, we became very good friends.

Doris was waiting in the room when I arrived, and we fell into each other's arms, full of love and new resolutions to stay sober. Of course, we didn't. Time after time, one or both of us would start drinking and not be able to stop. We were told by social workers, alcoholic specialists, institutional personnel, AA friends—almost everyone with whom we came in contact—that we'd never be able to stay off booze unless we separated. Our answer was always the same: we'd either make it together or go down together. Neither of us had anything else and, despite our lapses, we both knew we would die without each other. No matter how bad things were, no matter how discouraged we became, no matter how often we fell back into our old alcoholic patterns, we not only never discussed separation, but never even thought of it. Doris had gotten me off drugs. We might fall on our faces a thousand times along the way, but sooner or later we would get each other off booze.

We were on Skid Row nearly a year, from April, 1965, to February, 1966, during which period we rarely stayed sober for more than ten days or two weeks after leaving various institutions, jails, or hospitals. Each time, after the first, that I voluntarily entered Bridgewater, Doris checked herself into the Framingham Women's Reformatory to dry out for fifteen days. In between, we spent dozens of single nights in jail cells, or did short stretches in small alcoholic centers. One of the few places you could enter and leave voluntarily without agreeing to stay a definite period of time was the Washingtonian House, a famous old Jamaica Plain institution that may have been the first one in the nation set up specifically to help alcoholics. There, you were given paraldehyde, which prevents convulsions and D.T.'s, and permitted to leave whenever you pleased. Once, Doris was there three times in one week. Sometimes we went together. Other times, we managed to save enough money to go into a private hospital together for three or four days.

It was on one of those occasions that I had the worst case of the D.T.'s I can remember. Doris and I had been on a short bout, just a few days, when we decided to get into a hospital before we went broke on wine. On my second night there, I started to see objects across the room that were vibrating in rhythmic motion. One was a leering monkey, hanging on a stand beside the bed of a patient sleeping opposite from me. The monkey wouldn't stand still, and that bothered me, even though I knew it wasn't there. I closed my eyes to block it out, but when I opened them there it was, still grinning its horrible grin as it swayed back and forth.

When I turned away from the monkey, I saw ugly faces coming at me, and when I turned away from them there was a woman in white standing on a bedside table, her face insanely blank, her body slowly moving in many directions. Wherever I looked there was something upsetting—the monkey, the ugly faces, the woman in white. Knowing that I had the D.T.'s, I went to the desk and asked the attendant for more medication. Sometimes rest will stop the D.T.'s, but I hadn't slept for three nights before coming into the hospital or on my first night there. I had already had too much medicine, and the attendant's orders were not to give me any more. Returning to bed, I spent the night in and out of D.T.'s, hardly daring to open my eyes, for there were always the swaying monkey, the ugly faces, and the moving woman.

In the morning light the hallucinations weren't so vivid, but there was a lot of color distortion. When I asked the doctor to give me something, he told me that, since I was leaving the next day, he didn't dare. I said that I had spent the night in D.T.'s, was still hallucinating, and feared that the hallucinations would continue, but he still refused to give me more medication. By early afternoon, as I sat on a screened porch with Doris, I fell into a completely delusory and hallucinatory state. Out on a vacant lot behind the screen there seemed to be a field trial of pointer dogs. I saw the dogs, plain as could be, let loose, two at a time, beyond a patch of brush. It was a very calm, very real hallucination. I watched the dogs go on pointing and the trainer come in and look for the bird, something that is done in all such trials. When I saw the trainer shoot a blank pistol in the air and commented on it, I couldn't understand why nobody else could see or hear it. When the field trials ended, there was a parade of animals swaying like the monkey I had seen the night before, an endless procession that must have included every animal Noah had in his ark. I watched the parade all afternoon, and didn't believe Doris when she told me that I had been hallucinating since 12:00. But these were pleasant hallucinations, not at all like the terrible visions I had had the previous night. Or the worse ones that came the next night.

They started with the same monkey, but now he was slowly descending from the stand, that awful, leering grin still on his face as his body swelled and shrank in accordion movements while he approached me. I turned away from him and saw a sea of hairy black faces, zooming in on me like livestock on stampede. When I closed my eyes, I heard voices. One was Doris's, carrying on a conversation with a man. I couldn't figure out where they were, but suddenly I heard her crying upstairs. I stood on a chair to hear more clearly;

the man was trying to attack her, and she was crying and screaming. I jumped out of bed, ran out to the attendant and the nurse on duty, and told them someone was trying to rape my wife, but they refused to come down to my room to listen. I tried all the doors to get upstairs to Doris, but they were all locked. Back in my room, I could still hear her screaming and crying, so I went to the desk and begged the people there to do something. They told me that Doris was asleep in the women's section at the other end of the hall, but I didn't believe them. I kept going out every ten or fifteen minutes, until the attendant and the nurse finally came to my room. I couldn't understand why they didn't hear anything, why they didn't do anything, why they just looked at each other. I guess one of them said, "He's got the D.T.'s." The nurse turned to me, patted my arm and said in a soft voice, "Don't worry, your wife is safe in her own bed and nobody is bothering her." But all night long I heard her crying and the sounds of struggling in the room upstairs.

With the coming of daylight, I heard something hit the ground. I ran to the window, looked out, saw Doris lying on the grass crying, and was certain she had been thrown out of a second-floor window. I went to the desk and told the attendants that if they had done something during the night this wouldn't have happened. As I was begging them to go out and do something for her, or at least to let me do so, Doris came along the hallway. When they asked her if she was all right, she said, "Fine. I'm going to make a phone call." Puzzled, unable to figure out what was happening, I followed her to the phone booth and heard her telling a Catholic nun that I had set a lot of fires the day before. When she came out of the booth, I asked her why she had said those things, because she knew they weren't true, and she denied saying them.

As we walked down the hall, I saw the regular doctor coming toward me with about six attendants. He told me that I was in D.T.'s and said he'd give me heavy medication, then asked if I would go into the seclusion room, which I agreed to do. Once there, I took the medicine and slept for eight hours. When I woke up, everything was clear, and I could distinguish the real from the imaginary. I later learned that Doris wasn't talking to a nun, but to the hospital superintendent, and that she said nothing about my having set fires, but was committing me for fifteen days. Although still sick herself, she was planning to go to work to pay for my continued stay in the hospital. But the next day, when she came to see me and could tell that I was all right, she signed me out, which can be done anytime at a private hospital, even with a commitment.

All this happened several years ago, but the details are as vivid in my mind today as they were then. This is the horrible thing about the D.T.'s—the alcoholic remembers everything, good and bad. Hallucinations last anywhere from a few minutes to a lifetime. The prognosis is always guarded, because no one knows when the victim will recover. Some never do. Mental hospitals are full of people who have suffered D.T.'s for years, cemeteries crowded with the bodies of people who died in that condition.

During one of our sober periods, Doris phoned her sister and learned that her divorce had come through. Her sister sent the papers to us in care of a restaurant where Doris was a waitress and I a dishwasher. By the time the papers had arrived, we had enough money to get married. We took a bus to Nashua, because New Hampshire then had no waiting period as Massachusetts did. It was a really ecumenical wedding: Doris is Catholic, I'm Protestant, and the justice of the peace who performed the ceremony was Jewish.

We slipped just once more before leaving the South End for good. That was when we were on what must have been a ten-day bout before Doris went to Framingham and I to Bridgewater, both voluntarily, for the last time. By then John Metevier, the Bridgewater chief social worker, was accustomed to arranging for me to help handle the drug addicts after I came out of withdrawal. There were only a few addicts there, usually committed by a judge. When John introduced me to one, he would always tell him that I was a junkie who had been off the stuff for two years.

Once, during that last stay there, a junkie said, "Gee, doc, how did you ever kick two or three grains of morphine every two hours?"

"The wrong way, I guess," I said. "Otherwise, you and I wouldn't be sitting on the same bed."

I thought about that conversation often during my final stay at Bridgewater. Obviously, I hadn't kicked drugs the right way; certainly using alcohol as a substitute wasn't. And, for the first time, really, I could get the whole picture into proper focus. Doris and I weren't a couple of lost souls on the bum anymore. We were married, we loved each other, and we had to find a good life together. We couldn't do it on Skid Row. We had hit bottom and stayed there a long time. Now there was nowhere for us to go but up, and I made up my mind, once and for all, that that was the direction we were going to take.

XIV

W<small>HEN</small> I came out of Bridgewater and Doris left Framingham for the last time, our good resolutions sounded the same
as all our previous ones. How many times had we said,
"Never again"? How many times had we said, "This time
we'll make it"? How many times had we held each other
close and whispered, "We'll stop, we've got to stop"?

And how many times had we told each other, "Just a
couple of drinks to relax. That's all. Nobody can take this
pounding without relaxing. . ."?

For me to say that I provided the motivation to quit
would be as inaccurate as to say that Doris did. We both
knew how lucky we had been in not having to go to Bridgewater or Framingham by order of the court (that could have
meant two years or more behind bars or under guard). We
had always gone in voluntarily, stayed our fifteen days, and
come out. We both knew guards, attendants, doctors and
fellow patients (or prisoners) so well that we were greeted as
old friends every time we returned to dry out. We were wryly
welcomed on each arrival, expected back on each departure.
Social workers, welfare people, cops, jail guards, South End
habitués, nurses, doctors, hospital staff members, personnel
in the Washingtonian and other such places, judges, AA
groups, clergymen all over Greater Boston—all knew the

DeWitts, the big guy with the big thirst and the bad back, and his tall, blue-eyed wife whose thirst matched his own.

"They ought to separate," people said. "They'll never make it any other way. One starts and the other automatically goes along."

Doris was as well-known as I at Bridgewater, and I as familiar as she at Framingham. At Bridgewater, people asked for her, at Framingham they asked for me. Once, when a Bridgewater guard asked about Doris and I told him she was at Framingham, he said, "Jeez, doc, don't you think that's carrying this togetherness business a little too far?"

Perhaps it was. We were drunks, winos, bums, guttersnipes, the dregs of humanity's dregs. We were sick, miserable, slobbering, sniveling ciphers, swaying regulars on every queue lining up for free food, free shelter, free clothing, free money. We were prime candidates for oblivion, our nerves shattered, our livers enlarged, the days of our lives numbered. We were out of touch with our loved ones and they with us. All we had was each other. Sober, we could only hope and cry for our children. Drunk, we couldn't even hope, and when we cried it was as much for ourselves as for those we loved and wanted so desperately.

We didn't even like the taste of alcohol. We had to hold our breath and sometimes our noses to keep it down, and once it was down it ate into our entrails and kept us from eating, sleeping, sitting still, walking straight, reading, thinking, listening, talking sense, making love. The world was a fog and whatever we saw through it was double, triple, multiple. Days and weeks ran together until one of us had the sense or the strength to go where we could dry out—and resume drinking another day.

I had tried to escape through drugs before knowing Doris; she, before knowing me, through booze. After she had helped me out of the drug stage, I joined her on the booze route. Of course, neither drugs nor booze worked. Nor did punishment, the long days, nights, and months in jails and hospitals and mental institutions. I have never heard of an addict or an alcoholic dropping his addiction for fear of more punishment. All that does is to keep him off while serving his time; once out, he resumes his addiction.

I can't put my finger on exactly what set us on the right road back. Somewhere deep inside, we found concrete motivation to form concrete goals. AA helped, for as I pointed out before, it emphasizes the positive rather than the negative, and its twelve steps mention alcohol only once. It teaches the renewal of belief in a power greater than man—a lesson it took us years to learn. Doris had once been a good Catholic, I a good Protestant. We called the power in which we believed "God," but it took AA to teach us how very much in His hands we both were. We had taken Him for granted. We had prayed to Him, and let it go at that. For us—for any addict or alcoholic—that wasn't enough. We had to help Him help us. We had to know where we were going, and find the way ourselves. God could do only so much. Even He couldn't do more without our cooperation, and we hadn't been cooperating. We had to stop running away from reality, to stop trying to escape our obligations to God, ourselves, each other, our loved ones, humanity. We were intelligent people, with good educations, something to offer, something to give, too much to waste in the gutters of the South End. We weren't at the end of a road where there is no turning back—only at the bottom of a barrel. We *could* climb out if we tried, and after those last trips to Bridgewater and Framingham, we both seemed to realize this.

We understood, at last, that we had to exchange drugs and booze for a positive approach to our need for escape. The substitute had to be a number of things—good living, happiness, purgation of the traumas of our lives. We had to learn to cope, to stop worrying, to forget yesterday's or tomorrow's problems and concern ourselves only with today's. *There's nothing I can do about the past and I have no way of predicting the future, but I can, if I will, control the present.*

AA's precepts alone are not enough, but they help. They offer alcoholics frequent contact with people similarly afflicted. Because these people are aware of what happened to them as active alcoholics, they understand each other. Instead of putting up a front, they bring their personalities out into the open. They can handle their problems by being completely frank before the problems build up to the search for an escape route—booze for alcoholics, drugs for a junkie. AA's method is effective for both types of addict—interchangeably. Alcoholics can stay off booze as well by working with drug addicts as with other alcoholics; addicts can stay off drugs as well by working with alcoholics as with other addicts. Today, Doris and I work with addicts, which keeps me off drugs and both of us off booze. But getting here wasn't easy and staying here still isn't, and never will be. No matter how long I've been clean and both of us dry, we could slip back any time. Maybe we would if we lost our belief in God, if we harked back to the past or dreaded the future instead of concentrating upon getting through today. And we almost surely would if we separated. To this day, I have uneasy moments when I must walk fast with Doris by my side to overcome an urge for narcotics. And to this day, each of us must stop the other from surrendering to booze as an escape.

We didn't reach the turnoff from the long road to hell overnight. We each slipped a few times after those last stops at Bridgewater and Framingham. All that saved us was our faith in God, each other, and our determination to stop seeking escape in booze. I don't know how often we slipped after February, 1966, when we left those institutions for good—maybe four, five, half a dozen times. Once, I was falsely accused of beating Doris. Another time we were arrested and nearly sentenced, I to Bridgewater and she to Framingham, but an understanding judge gave us a break when he was shown that we were trying and apparently on the verge of success.

In nearly every case, I was the first to start drinking, and every time I started, Doris joined me. One of us always became lucid enough to keep these drinking bouts down to a minimum—I think the longest lasted about a week. Once Doris had the D.T.'s and hallucinated about an apartment we had taken. She imagined herself hiding in a closet because the rooms were wired and everyone could hear whatever we said; she thought that people were watching her on television. I had a doctor give her medication, which calmed her, so that I was able to sit down and talk to her about it. She could accept the fact that I was right, but kept on hallucinating. I took her to an AA meeting that night to get her out of the apartment, because sometimes you can stop hallucinations by changing the victim's environment. In that case, it didn't work, but I gave her enough medication to put her to sleep when we got home, and the next morning she was all right.

Well-meaning people continued to tell us to separate, but we stuck together and fought together. It wasn't easy. Many a night we turned the clock's face to the wall so that we wouldn't know what time the liquor stores closed. Many a night one of us had an urge to drink and the other softly, never harshly nor angrily, talked until the urge went away. We kept looking for things to do, people to help, old contacts to re-establish. We corresponded with my parents, with friends in Maine, with Doris's sister. We missed our children, but knew where they were and what they were doing, all but Karen, who had run away. I worried about Karen, prayed for her, and hoped for the day that I would hear from her. My parents kept in touch with the orphanage where the three younger ones were, and they assured me that all, including Doug with his diabetic necessities, were doing well.

In 1966, while I was still working as a janitor and after I had been dry for several months, I wrote to the Massachusetts Board of Registration for Medicine, asking for the proper papers to apply for a license to practice. I had never practiced in Massachusetts, but could have, since before leaving medical school I had passed the National Board exams that are accepted by nearly all states, including Massachusetts. Now I really thought I was ready, but when I saw the application, I knew I couldn't fill it out. *Have you ever lost your license?*, it asked. *Where? Under what conditions? Have you ever been arrested on narcotics charges? Have you ever been addicted to drugs or alcohol?*

If I told the truth, as I knew I must, all the answers would have been wrong. And if the Board demanded a personal interview, as I was sure it would, its interviewers would see a craggy-faced, beaten-up man looking far older than his years, working as a janitor. I put the application in a drawer and not long after that went on another bout with Doris.

But that and the other times we became drunk were isolated incidents that only temporarily delayed our comeback from Skid Row. Before, these bouts had formed the pattern of our lives. Now our pattern was the long road back. That began at halfway houses immediately after a young priest from the Cathedral picked up Doris in Framingham and me in Bridgewater to take us back to Boston. He had arranged in advance for Doris to go to a halfway house in Jamaica Plain and I to one in the South End. Both were run by private individuals, alcoholics working with alcoholics. The one I stayed in was very good. The guy who started it had been on and off Skid Row for years. I think he had once been a mechanical engineer. With the help of friends, for he had nothing when he started, he bought a South End slum house and fixed it up. Through welfare, he found jobs for his patients and money to help care for them.

I went through the typical procedure there, staying about three weeks until I had saved enough money from dishwashing jobs to leave. Doris did the same. We kept in touch with each other, and when we left the halfway houses, we took a room in Jamaica Plain, which, although part of Boston, is far enough away from the South End to spare us any unpleasant memories. I worked as a janitor in a nursing home, and Doris had a job in a hotel replacing broken light bulbs. After about three months we had saved enough to buy a couple of nurse uniforms for her, and she got a hospital job. We both stayed dry for six months, but when we slipped we didn't go completely off the deep end. Our drinking lasted only a couple of days; we kept our jobs by calling in sick, and got off booze by going to AA meetings.

A few weeks later I was promoted to nurse's aide, because the people for whom I worked knew, by then, that I could do more than mop floors, carry out garbage, and take care of furnaces. They didn't know I was a doctor, and never asked. Nobody asks questions under those circumstances. They hire you, you do your job, and that's the end of it. Maybe they can tell by your manner of speech that you are educated, but they assume you don't want to talk about your past—and in my case, they were right. But when I became a nurse's aide— my first job in nearly two years that paid more than a dollar and a quarter an hour—I was terribly humiliated because I had to take orders from nurses. Normally, of course, it's the other way around: the doctor gives the orders and the nurses carry them out. I slipped once during that period, but again got back on my feet quickly enough to save my job.

Between the two of us, Doris and I finally managed to pay for the apartment in Jamaica Plain where she later had the D.T.'s and hallucinated. It was big, old, and pretty shabby, but it looked like a castle to us. We scrubbed and cleaned and painted until it gleamed. Through AA friends, we picked up furniture from someone who was going to give it to the Morgan Memorial, which would have passed it along to people such as us anyway. When it was all fixed up, we invited my parents to visit us. I had been ashamed to write to them when we were on Skid Row, but now I was in constant touch with them. Only after I left the halfway house did I let them know where I was and that Doris and I were married. They already knew about Doris, but hadn't met her. She was a little nervous about inviting them, but I wasn't. They had gone through all the years of drug hell with me, and they had fought the Skid Row months with me in their hearts. Even though Doris and I had nearly gone down the drain together, they knew she was my anchor, my one hope for a normal life and a reunion with my children. They respected her and admired her fighting spirit, which had helped to bring both of us out of the depths. After what we had been through, for my parents to be able to visit us in a home of our own was as much a source of pride to them as to us. We were still struggling, but on our way up, and to my parents Doris was not just my wife, but my partner in the struggle.

Doris was more worried than I about whether or not they would accept her. On the day we expected them, she bought a blueberry pie on her way home from work, but when she arrived there was already one on the table. We had left the door unlocked in case they arrived while we were both working. My mother told Doris that she had bought a rolling pin and pie plates because we didn't have any, and had made the pie herself. Doris quietly put hers on a shelf in the cabinet to avoid hurting my mother's feelings. Their relationship was wonderful right from the start, as it continued up to my mother's death, and as it still continues between Doris and my father. I told them about the pie before they left for Skowhegan to see my sister, and we all got a big kick out of it.

About three months after I started working as a nurse's aide, I took a state job as a laboratory technician in Jamaica Plain. I had always hated lab work, but not as much as I hated taking orders from nurses. Besides, this was a better-paying job, and I decided to stay with it for at least a year so that I could establish a work pattern.

When we woke up on Christmas morning, 1967, Doris, who had bought a small turkey and all the fixings, said, "Honey, even though it isn't much of a turkey, we can't possibly eat it all ourselves. What do you think about going down to the South End and bringing some poor guy home to share it with us?"

I thought it was a great idea. I took the trolley to the subway and the rapid transit up to East Berkeley Street, and ambled around. I half hoped to see someone I knew, but it was a cold day and very few people were outside. I finally found a man sitting on a stoop—bleary-eyed, drooling, his clothes filthy—and started to walk past him. Then I thought, *This is just the kind of guy who needs a decent meal. Doris and I were that way once.* I turned back and shook him gently by the shoulder, and when he looked up I said, "How about coming home and having a real Christmas dinner with me?"

"Christmas dinner . . . ?"

He slurred the words, but his dull eyes lit up enough to make me pretty sure that I had gotten through to him.

"My wife and I were once on the bum just like you," I said, "Now we're okay and have plenty to eat. Come share it with us."

He shook his head, and through the fog of his speech I caught something to the effect of, "Who would want a bum like me to Christmas dinner?" I told him that we would, and helped him to his feet, then led him back to the rapid transit. Only after we had changed in the subway to a Jamaica Plain trolley did he begin to perk up. He didn't talk much, but he kept wiping the spittle from his lips, and he was smiling when we got off at the stop nearest our apartment. When we arrived, Doris greeted him like an old friend, telling him how glad she was to see him and how much we appreciated his coming into our home on Christmas day. I took him into the bathroom and helped him out of his clothes and into the shower, while Doris got him some fresh clothes. He was about six inches shorter than I and she had to cut down the pant legs and shirt sleeves, but the entire outfit didn't look bad on him. In the meantime, I shaved him and combed his hair, and when he came out he looked like a different guy. Although still unsteady, he spoke and acted differently, too.

We were all kindred souls for the afternoon, three alcoholics who understood each other as only fellow alcoholics can. We ate around midafternoon, and he got everything down. When he began to get edgy, Doris talked softly to him, telling him that if we could come back anybody could. She didn't seem to make much progress, nor did I when I tried. But we hadn't brought him in to try to "save a soul blighted by alcohol." We had brought him in for the sheer pleasure of doing something for somebody else. This was the essence of our own resolve, the salvation of our own future. When he thanked us and told us he had to leave, I gave him a few dollars. He had a choice of spending them on booze or on a room, with enough left over for transportation to find work the next day. We didn't tell him what to do, and it was a year before we learned what he actually did do.

On the following Christmas we got a card from him with a ten-dollar bill enclosed and a note saying that he hadn't had a drink since he had seen us.

Doris's last bout came in March, 1968. I don't know what had set her off—she was drinking when I arrived home from work. I didn't try to stop her, but I didn't join her either. We talked for a long time, practically all night, and the next day I stayed home from work and helped her help herself back to reality. From that day to this, neither of us has crossed the line away from sobriety.

Now we had our goal. If I could regain my medical license, we decided, we would concentrate upon victims of drug addiction. I had been working in the lab, and by now had stayed off liquor for a year and off drugs for three. I felt now that I was ready to fill out the application I had put away two years before—ready to answer all the questions truthfully, ready to face the State Board in person, ready to express my hope and desire to work with addicts. I had several strikes against me, but many things going for me, too. Nobody was better equipped to work with addicts. The very things that were held against me were my best qualifications for a field as baffling to medical science in 1968 as it had ever been. Addiction was incurable, as, to the best of my knowledge, it always will be. But there *were* ways to keep addicts off drugs, and I felt I knew—as I still do—what they were.

I went to the drawer and pulled out the questionnaire that had rested there for so long. I filled it out, knowing that my answers were the direct opposite of what they should have been. *Yes, I lost my license to practice in Maine. Yes, I have been arrested several times on alcohol and narcotics charges. I am addicted to both, but have used no drugs for three years and no alcohol for one.* Because the answers were all damning, I wrote a supplementary letter, which, in effect, said, "Here's my life, here's where I have been, here's where I am now, here's where I want to go." I wrote that I hoped to work with drug addicts, because I knew, from personal experience, what they were suffering, and I had realistic ideas about how to treat them. I also wrote of my concern about the rapidly growing rate of drug use among young people, with whom I would have a special rapport because of my background. And I wrote that Doris was a registered nurse who, although never addicted to drugs, was a nondrinking alcoholic like myself and would assist me in my work.

Now we had to wait for a reply. This was a period of great anxiety, one that once would have probably driven us both to drink. I wanted to get it over with, yet couldn't visualize how I would succeed on any oral exam. I had to sell the Board the fact that my addictive history was an asset, not a liability, and this would be difficult. Very few medical boards are willing to accept any addiction as advantageous to a doctor because, addiction being incurable, it always threatens to erupt at any time.

The letter came a week after I sent in the application. Doris, who had been curiously unenthusiastic, stood beside me as I opened it. The answer was hopeful. The Board members would consider me, but wished to talk to me first. They set a date and time for me to appear before them.

"It's a start," I said.

"At least they didn't turn you down," said Doris. "Do you want me to go with you?"

"No. You'll be more uptight waiting for me to come out of the hearing than working."

"Okay, honey. I'll go to work." (She had a good job as a nursing supervisor.) "Call me at the hospital when you're through."

On the day of my appearance, which was at the JFK Building, I took the subway to Boston's new Government Center, arriving about 25 minutes ahead of time. I went into the building for a trial run, walking from the entrance up to the Board's offices. It took exactly two and a quarter minutes. I then went back downstairs and out into the street, for I still had about twenty minutes and didn't care to sweat them out in the waiting room.

I walked up the hill to the courthouse and thought, *That's where the "tombs" are.* It would be a pretty safe bet that only a small percentage of Bostonians know there is such a place as the "tombs"—the men's and women's overnight detention cells for criminals and drunks. Probably, a still smaller percentage know where it is, in the basement of the courthouse. Doris and I had been there many times, starting with the time I first came for her there when she was arrested right after we arrived in Boston. Even while sober, I had always felt tight little knots in my stomach whenever I passed the place. But this time it didn't happen. It was a good sign, for it meant that my nerves were steady. Later, after walking to the gold-domed State House, I turned and went slowly down the hill. On the way, I said a short prayer, Thy Will Be Done." I had said it every conscious day of my life since I was a little boy, and never had I said it more fervently. A medical license hanging on the wall of the Walpole State Prison would do me no good.

I had timed my return to the JFK Building correctly to the second, and now walked into the waiting room of the Board at the exact moment I was expected. A young lady also applying for a license was ahead of me, but she only stayed a few minutes. She was followed out by a secretary, who asked, "Are you Dr. DeWitt?" After I said, "Yes," she went into another room, then came back and told me that I could enter the Board room. In there was a long table at which were seated seven or eight men, one of whom pointed to an empty chair at the far end as he courteously invited me to sit down. While walking to my seat I thought how similar, yet how different, were those mental hospital meetings I had so dreaded and this interview. At those institutions, my freedom was riding on the way I answered challenging questions. I had a lot riding on this meeting, too, but I sensed a different mood here. The men in the hospitals were inclined to give me the worst of it. These men, although their eyes bored into me, seemed to want to give me a break, and their questions proved it.

I don't recall more than a casual comment about my past. Practically all the questions concerned my future. I told them that I hoped to work in the field of addiction, that I preferred junkie patients because addiction was spreading so rapidly among young people and so little was known about how to treat them. I said that the rate of success was too low (only about 5 percent) and that I thought I could contribute something toward raising it. Various members of the Board asked questions, and I answered them as simply and directly as I could. I was in there perhaps fifteen minutes, and I could tell by the way the men spoke and looked at me that I had made a good impression. When they told me that I could leave, the secretary, who saw me to the door, said, "You will hear from us very shortly, doctor."

Four days later, it was on a Saturday afternoon and both Doris and I were home, the letter came from the Board of Registration for Medicine. I stood looking at it for a long time, my fingers shaking, my insides tight, my back tingling. Beside me, Doris, who had shown no emotion before about the situation, now stood tense and waiting for me to open the envelope. I didn't look at her, but I felt her beside me while my eyes tried to penetrate the opaque object in my trembling hands.

If they intended to turn me down, I thought, *they would have used a different line of questioning. They would have asked more about my past and less about my future.* Then, as I looked at the envelope I turned it all around. *Maybe,* I thought, *they didn't want to ask about my past because they were too courteous to embarrass me. Maybe they felt they would embarrass themselves—a man with my record had disgraced an honored profession. It's easy to write a letter, so much easier than telling a man to his face that he would not be permitted to practice. "With your past, we just can't accept you."*

These thoughts flashed through my mind in seconds that seemed like hours. I had to open that letter to find the answer, for my whole future was there, inside that envelope. Suddenly, in one quick motion, I tore it open and spread out the contents in my two hands for Doris to read, since I was too tall for her to look over my shoulder. It was a very short letter, brief and beautiful:

"The decision of this Board is to grant you a license to practice medicine in the Commonwealth of Massachusetts as of the date you receive this letter."

When Doris and I turned to face each other, tears were running down her face and welling up in my eyes. Now, all the emotion she had been holding back for so long finally came to the surface. As we hugged, I could feel her shoulders shaking with sobs of joy. We stood this way for long minutes before we recovered enough equilibrium to talk.

"You're so happy," I said. "So excited. Tell me, honey, why didn't you show your feelings before?"

"I couldn't, Jim," she said. "I didn't dare be happy. You had planned too many things that didn't happen. You've never planned anything—not even Brandy Pond—with such hope in your heart. You never wanted anything, except your children, more than you wanted this. I couldn't stand seeing you get knocked down again. That's why I seemed so casual about this. I really wasn't—my nerves were as taut as yours. But I couldn't show it, couldn't encourage you, couldn't even hope with you. This time, I had to see it happen."

"And now it has."

"Yes, darling. Now it has. And now I can let go. I'm so proud—so very, very proud—of my doctor husband."

XV

UNTIL the early 1960s, Boston had never been noted as an especially easy place to get narcotics on the street. But in the years that followed, that city snowballed, until, by 1968 (when I regained my license to practice medicine and my federal license to dispense drugs), it led the country in illicit drug traffic. Much of the blame for this was placed on the so-called hippie invasion of the city that summer, but I don't think the hippies contributed heavily to the situation—it had been building for years. Greater Boston today is still probably the easiest place in the country to get anything, from marijuana and LSD to heroin, on the street.

Heroin usually is smuggled into the country in concentrated form, through a large seaport or airline terminal. In the East, most of the heroin goes first to New York, where it is cut, bagged, and sent up and down the coast. Although there's plenty of junk in other big eastern cities, the Greater Boston area is completely saturated with it. I would say perhaps 80 percent of the pushers are themselves addicts, who push to support their habit. They might, for example, buy $500 worth of heroin from a New York contact, cut it in two, use half themselves, and rebag the other half to peddle on the street for $500. In this way, they break even and still have enough to keep themselves in all the skag they need.

The first reaction of the casual observer is to say, "What are the police doing? They must know about this traffic. Why don't they stop it?"

In answer to that, I can say that of all the drug-plagued cities in the country, Boston (through the narcotics divisions of various police departments in and around the city) handles the problem as intelligently as any, if not more so. Its police learned long ago that addiction is a disease, not a crime. They're merciless, as they should be, when they pick up a nonusing pusher. I agree with the popular feeling that a non-addict who deliberately starts a young person on drugs should have the book thrown at him. But any user, pusher or otherwise, is sick and must be treated as a patient. Obviously, a pusher must be taken off the street, but at least he is motivated by the necessity of filling his own needs, not by the desire to bring clean kids into the drug scene to increase his clientele.

I do not condone pushing, or, for that matter, addiction. Nor am I easy on the addicts who come to me for treatment. On the contrary, I'm as tough as I have to be with them. My technique is simple, direct, and, in its own way, I suppose, merciless, although I prefer to call it humane.

I start by saying, "Don't try to con me. I'm a junkie my-self." I have to do that, because every active addict must be a con artist to get what he needs. I play it straight with all my patients, and I expect them all to play it straight with me. I give therapy, individually and in groups, the kind of psychiatric therapy that I believe is necessary in treating addicts. There is no section of the city, especially its northern environs (where Doris and I have been living since 1968), where I don't personally know most of the junkies and junkie-pushers. And I have contacts all over New England—in fact, in other parts of the country as well. This is not because I'm an exceptional doctor, but because I'm a junkie, and nobody can understand a junkie as well as another one.

In my treatment of patients, I trade heavily upon my own past. Sometimes I think it was worth all the anguish I went through, just to have reached the point where I am now. The authorities understand me, work with me, refer patients to me, and encourage me to lecture in ever-widening circles. The average record of keeping junkies clean for a year or more is about 3 percent; mine is about 10 percent, because I have convinced at least that many, and others who don't make it for a year, but who stay clean for months, that, while they will always be junkies, they *can* be helped. Sometimes I must work on them over the telephone. I know that nonusing addicts get cravings for junk; I do, to this day. My therapy is to walk with Doris. Often, theirs is to talk to me—or, at least, to call me so I can talk to them. This is basically the same therapy that alcoholics give each other in AA. Although not quite as successful, it, combined with the other therapy I employ, works better than any other treatment for addicts of which I know.

All the clinics, all the hospitals, all the sanitariums, all the Lexington, Kentuckys, in the world, still won't keep a junkie off junk indefinitely—only for as long as he is on the premises. Without motivation, he'll go back sooner or later. I try to give him motivation. I try to give him pride, self-respect, hope, a sense of belonging. I don't want him to be ashamed of his ailment, any more than I am ashamed of mine. I want to minimize for him the loneliness that all addicts feel; for, no matter how many people are around him, every addict is desperately lonely. He doesn't have to be, and won't be, if I can get through to him.

I believe withdrawal should be made as painless as possible.

There is no reason for an addict to go through the agony of cold turkey withdrawal. Some so-called experts (and there really aren't any experts, not even me, in this field) feel that long-term withdrawal should be endured, perhaps as a sort of punishment for addiction. I disagree. Being an addict is punishment enough for anyone. For withdrawal purposes, I'm a great believer in methadone. This is a fairly new synthetic, which, although addictive, can be controlled. I dispense it in small quantities designed for a ten-day withdrawal period. On the first day the addict gets eight 10-mg. tablets, enough for one day. On the second day he comes back, at which time, besides a psychiatric session, he receives eight more tablets, but uses only six, leaving him with two extras. When he returns the third day, he gets eight more, but saves two or three. Those extra tablets, plus the ten I give him on his fourth visit, enables him to take daily tablets in decreasing measure. By the time he returns to me on the tenth day, he will have used up all his tablets, a few less each day, finishing with half a tablet on the last day. In this way, he gets through an easy withdrawal from heroin, and is off methadone as well. I tell the patient exactly how much methadone he should take at a time, and when. Once he has completed that ten-day regimen, he gets no more drugs from me. Instead, he goes into group therapy, and if he keeps attending regularly, there's a pretty good chance that he can control his drug habit indefinitely.

One of the mistakes some doctors make is prescribing too much methadone at one time, so that the patient won't have to come back often. I know of regimens whereby a patient can obtain 45 tablets on one prescription, which is an invitation to disaster. Methadone can be exchanged for smaller quantities of heroin, and anything that can be exchanged for heroin is bad. Ten methadone tablets are useless to a pusher; 45 are something else again. If a pusher gets enough methadone, he can sell it in lieu of heroin, so he might swap with the addict under treatment, demanding a great deal more methadone for the heroin he'll give up. He can then make a profit on the methadone, for junkies hooked on it will settle for it if heroin is unavailable or too expensive.

The police, whom I once considered my enemies, are now my friends. Those who understand what I'm trying to do are especially good to me. Those who know me know that I will level with them, because we're all on the same team, trying to do the same thing. Those who don't know me learn quickly enough that they don't have to beat their brains out investigating me. All they have to do is ask.

Not long after I began my practice, which is almost exclusively with young addicts, I had a visit from four men who once would have scared me to death. One was Massachusetts State Police Sgt. Daniel L. Delaney, now in charge of special investigations of narcotics violations in the Commonwealth. He was then Zone Commander of the Northeastern Division of the State Police Narcotics Bureau. With him were Mal Kadra and Gil Frachette, State Police undercover agents, and an officer from the Manchester police department.

Delaney, a hard-bitten veteran of more than 15 years of narcotics investigation, was there in response to a complaint lodged against me for violating laws by prescribing and dispensing narcotics to drug addicts. After identifying himself and his companions, he said, "Are you treating drug addicts in your home?"

"That's right."

"Are you running a so-called clinic in your home?"

"I have patients coming to my home regularly. You can call it a clinic, if you wish."

Delaney, who was used to evasive answers from people he investigated, looked surprised.

"You mean you admit it?" he said.

"I'm not ashamed of it, Sergeant," I replied. "I'm a junkie who's been clean for more than three years and an alcoholic who hasn't had a drink in two years. I'm also a doctor who once was deprived of his medical license and his federal license to write prescriptions. Both were returned to me through the efforts of people who had enough confidence in me to give me another chance."

"Do you keep records of your patients?"

"Yes."

"May I see them?"

"Certainly," I said.

Now Dan Delaney was really surprised. I called Doris, introduced her to him and his colleagues, and asked her to open our records to them.

"Dr. DeWitt," Delaney said, "this is the first time any doctor dispensing narcotics has ever let me examine his records without objections. Most of these doctors talk about professional ethics in keeping the confidences of their patients, and we have to get court orders to see what they're doing."

"I have nothing to hide," I said. "I'm not breaking any law. I'm doing the job the way I think it should be done. If you find anything wrong, tell me and I'll change—provided that you're sure it *is* wrong."

Delaney thumbed through my files, then turned to me and said, "There's nothing wrong here. In fact, I've never seen so much that was right. Would you mind telling me how you treat your people?"

"When they come in to me I lay it right on the line," I said. "I tell them I will help them, but only if they have the guts to kick the habit. I don't believe in pampering them. I tell them right away that it won't be easy, that they might slip, that addiction is incurable but controllable, and that, because I am a junkie, I won't give them any medication directly—I don't keep any in the house. Frankly, Sergeant, I'm afraid to—I don't trust myself. I need therapy as much as my patients do. So does my wife who, like me, is a non-drinking alcoholic. We find that helping these kids helps us."

Then Delaney began firing his questions faster. He demanded more information about my methods of treatment, what drugs I prescribed, how I knew whether or not a junkie was conning me. When he asked that, I grinned and said, "As an active junkie, I had to be a con man. If you've had much experience in this field, you know one junkie can't con another." At least they think they can't.

Delaney grinned back, and his whole attitude softened.

"You're right, doctor," he said. "But I've seen so many doctors who, in trying to treat junkies, get conned to death. Even when a doctor is strictly on the level, trying to do an honest job of rehabilitation and treatment, he can be conned out of all sorts of drugs because he's sorry for his patient."

The narcotics officer and the men with him must have spoken with me for three hours. When we were through, Delaney said, "I believe you're doing a good job. If anyone tries to pressure you into writing prescriptions for them, call me and I'll help straighten them out."

"I will call you from time to time," I said, "but it won't be for that. I'm a junkie and have junkie friends. I'm sure that if anything like that happens, I can handle it myself."

"Fine," Dan said. "I don't think you're violating the law in any way. I'll say so in my report answering the complaint against you. You make sense. The combination of your background and experience in narcotics and your medical and psychiatric work through the years is unbeatable."

I know that Dan investigated me to make sure I wasn't conning him, and I know what he was told. Every junkie to whom he talked on the North Shore had heard of me, swore by me, and assured him that I couldn't be conned. At least two were patients of mine. One was a boy who had been in trouble with the police for years. I kept him clean for four months, and, when he came back, got him started on the right road again.

There's no real secret of success in this business, no guarantee that anything will work. In drug addiction, one clean year is compared to five healthy years for a former cancer patient. If an addict can stay clean for a year, it means he has a chance to stay clean forever, just as, if a cancer patient has no trouble for five years, he's considered cured.

But therein lies the difference. Most cancer patients remain in good health for many years if they can last for five. But drug addicts might go back any time. The one-year rule in addiction is only for statistical purposes. I've been clean more than a year several times, but I didn't stop until I had motivation—in my case, Doris gave me the desire to live a normal life and helped me over my drug bumps, as she still does. True, we hit the booze together and had a terrible time coming back, but we finally did make it. Neither of us has touched alcohol since Doris's last short bout in 1968.

I'll never be out of the woods altogether, never be cured of addiction, probably never break even with the world financially. I have collected very little in fees since I began working with young addicts. So much depends upon their faith in me that I can't even go to rich parents for fees unless the addict himself takes me to them, and few do. These kids, rich and poor, don't want their parents to know about their illness, and I have to respect their confidence. If I don't, they'll stop coming to me and be back on drugs within a week. Most are, anyway. After all, when I say I have 35 percent success with my patients (30 percent higher than the national average) I'm also saying I have 65 percent failure. It's like a ballplayer's batting average. A .300 hitter gets three hits in ten times at bat. He fails on his other seven trips to the plate. But a consistent .300 hitter in the major leagues is still considered an outstanding star.

I still have personal problems; only my oldest child Karen, is back with me. The other three—Doug, Dana and Julie—are still in the Tennessee orphanage where they had been sent when Kay found it impossible to care for them. They have all been with me at various times over the summer, but at this writing I still can't afford to support them properly for the rest of the year.

After Karen ran away from Atlanta, she spent some time there and in New Orleans. Then she became seriously ill. At that point, she asked for me, and I had a call from her New Orleans doctor. Since joining Doris and me, she has made a complete about-face and is now going to North Shore Community College in Beverly, near our apartment in Gloucester. We are as close now as back in the days when I used to take her hunting in the Maine woods, and she regards Doris as a mother and big sister combined. The two are members of a mutual admiration society. My other children and Doris get along well. Our ambition and hope is that some day my four children and Doris's two can all live under the same roof.

I can think of no better way to close than to quote excerpts from a speech I gave at the Massachusetts Police Narcotics School in Quincy, Massachusetts, in the autumn of 1970. Among other things, here is what I said:

> I was asked by the Attorney General's office to speak here tonight on the disease of drug dependency. Some of you who know a little about my past life must realize the tremendous satisfaction that fills me, at this

moment, knowing that for the next hour you ladies and gentlemen are to be my captive audience instead of me yours.

While sitting here surrounded by narcotics law enforcement officers, I was struck by the full meaning of the word 'transformation.' A very short time ago I would have sworn to myself on all that is holy that I would never reveal even a glimpse of the life I led, first as an active narcotics addict wherever I happened to be and then as an active alcoholic, which landed me on Boston's Skid Row for a year. The transformation came when I realized that only by rewalking that road to hell could I truly help others, and this is why I am here today.

Within the past two years I watched a 'dishonorably' infectious disease move into my area of the world with such speed and destructive force that it reached epidemic proportions, as it has elsewhere in the country. In spite of this, many people are still trying to deny that this is true or that drug addiction is a disease at all. To give proof of both, I need only to point out that 104 heroin addicts have sat down with me individually and collectively in my living room *during the past four days.* They walked, hitchhiked, or drove to get to my house out in the country, because some junkie told them at different times in different places that a recovered junkie doctor was willing to try to help them.

This was not in Boston, but in Gloucester—104 young people in four days, all hooked on heroin, all wanting to get off. Multiply those 104 by the infinitely larger numbers of addicts in Greater Boston and other metropolitan areas of the nation, and you will see what I mean when I say this disease has reached epidemic proportions.

The faces of these boys and girls, giving out an almost hopeless cry for help, has supplied my motivating force to take off all the protective cloaks I've worn to hide the scars I received on the pathological road that is guaranteed to the victim of the disease of drug addiction. I traveled those roads with narcotics, amphetamines, barbiturates, and booze. I found they all led to the same hospitals, jails, and courts, and that the bumps along the way robbed me of everything I had wanted in life.

How do I know a girl or boy can keep this disease under control? Because I'm here right now to prove it. I am my own best example. Believe me, if I could lick this, anybody could.

I was not trying to con these fledgling students of the narcotics scene, but shooting straight with them. Addiction to anything—drugs or alcohol—may never be cured, but *can* be kept under control. People who can't smoke quit using tobacco. People allergic to penicillin never take it. Diabetics don't eat sugar. And addicts can be taught to spurn drugs or liquor.

It's not easy, but it's not impossible. Anything that's not impossible can be done. It takes guts, will power, motivation, and desire, on the part of the addict. It takes knowledge, patience, toughness, understanding, and cooperation, on the part of those who want to help him.

And on both sides of the fence, it takes faith—faith in God, faith in oneself, faith in the future. I know. I've traveled the road to hell—both ways.